To Brother _____,
A valued s_ _____
and Man _____
There are no shortcuts to
any place worth going. The
happiest people don't
necessarily have the best of
everything, they just make
the most of the things that
they have. Every moment is
opportunity, focus on what's
important, capture the good
time, do away with negativity
and if things don't work out,
take a chance, review your
attitude until things improve.
Never give up, no matter how
you feel. Get up, show up
but never give up. Life isn't
about weathering the storm.
It's about learning how to
dance in the rain. Against
all odds when failure is not an
option   Leo Dicks June 16, 2016

AGAINST ALL ODDS
—4TH DOWN AND FOREVER

*How the 1970 Marshall University
Football Team Plane Crash Inspired Me*

LESTER BRIAN HICKS

Lester B Hicks

PO Box 51, 4644 Powder Springs Dallas Road
Powder Springs, GA 30127
www.authorlesterbrianhicks.com
Phone: (678) 469 - 5273

Published by **Lester B Hicks**   *05/07/2014*

ISBN:1511841567
ISBN:9781511841566

Against all Odds—4th Down and Forever:

How the 1970 Marshall University Football Team Plane Crash Inspired Me

Despite seemingly insurmountable odds, Les Hicks was able to achieve success in life as well as great spiritual growth. As one of fourteen children in a family of sharecroppers, his aspirations for education seemed laughable, but my father refused to let his poverty-stricken childhood define his children's futures. He worked tirelessly to defy the stereotypes of African American males and proved to himself and all the naysayers that he could achieve the American dream and inspire others along the way.

The turning point of Les' life came after the Marshall University plane crash in 1970; that's when he realized how precious life is and not to take another moment for granted. This pivotal moment changed the course of his life and guided him to his incredibly bright future. Les' journey echoes the universal sentiment that you can beat the odds as long as you have faith, determination, and discipline and tirelessly pursue happiness.

This book takes readers on an insightful ride of heartbreak, triumph, and perseverance. In a time of despair, division, and recession, a book like this is just what the doctor ordered because it's relatable and its message of hope and generosity transcends race, gender, and age (Tiffany Hicks).

Les dedicates this book to his parents, George and Clifford Hicks, who were born in southern Georgia. His mother gave birth to seven girls and seven boys on a plantation on which they toiled as sharecroppers during the early 1900s. Les Hicks was the twelfth of these hardworking, spiritual, and honest people. Those attributes were instilled in Hicks gave honor to his parents.

ACKNOWLEDGMENTS

I give honor to the 1970 Marshall University football team crash victims who gave me inspiration to write this book over forty-three years after they perished. The loss of their lives has affected mine in ways that I never deemed imaginable. Southern Airways Flight 932, en route from Kinston, North Carolina to Huntington, West Virginia, crashed into a hill just short of the airport with the loss of all seventy-five people on board. The plane was carrying thirty-six members of the Marshall University Thundering Herd football team, five members of the coaching staff, twenty-four boosters, five crew and five Marshall support staff members.

The Marshall University Football Coaching Staff:

Rick Tolley (head coach), Deke Brackett, Al Carelli, Jr., Frank Loria, and Jim Moss

The 1970 Marshall University Football Team Crash Victims:

Jim Adams, Mark Andrews, Michael Blake, Dennis Blevins, Willie Bluford, Larry Brown, Thomas Brown, Roger Childers, Stuart Cottrell, Rick Dardinger, David DeBord, Kevin Gilmore, David Griffith, Art Harris, Bob Harris, Bobby Hill, Joe Hood, Tom Howard, Marcello Lajterman, Rick Lech, Barry Nash, Pat Norrell, Bob Patterson, Scottie Reese, Jack Repasy, Larry Sanders, Al Saylor, Art Shannon, Ted Shoebridge, Allen Skeens,

Jerry Stainback, Robert VanHorn, Roger Vanover, Freddy Wilson, John Young, and Tom Zborill.

Team Support Staff:
Gary George, Charles Kautz, Gene Morehouse, Jim Schroer, and Donald Tackett.

Devoted Fans:
Charles Arnold, Rachel Arnold, Donald Booth, Dr. Joseph Chambers, Peggy Chambers, Shirley Ann Hagley, Dr. Ray Hagley, Arthur Harris Sr., Emmett Heath, Elaine Heath, Cynthia Jarrell, James Jarrell, Kenneth Jones, Jeff Nathan, Brian O' Connor, Michael Prestera, Dr. Glenn Preston, Phyllis Preston, Courtney Proctor, Dr. Herbert Proctor, Helen Ralsten, Murrill Ralsten, Parker Ward, and Norman Weichmann.

Southern Airways Flight Crew:
Captain Frank Abbott, Danny Deese, Charlene Poat, Jerry Smith, and Patricia Vaught.

The loss of all these lives made me take a closer look at my own life because Marshall University recruited me when I was a senior in high school. If I had qualified academically and accepted a scholarship from Marshall, I would have been on the team. I would not have been on the flight because freshman didn't travel with varsity during that era. I thank God for not allowing me to experience a tragic event of this magnitude firsthand.

1970 Marshall University Crash Victims:
Death does not respect anyone. There are no guarantees we will live to see tomorrow. From November 14, 1970, to the present, I made a commitment to pray as if I were going to die tomorrow and to work as if I were going to live forever. Since that November night, I have lived by that promise except for one lonely, dark night, when I considered suicide, but Nick Diniaco gave me hope for the future.

Nick, a longtime friend, mentor, and confidant, told me that each player, coach, fan, and booster on that flight would have loved to have had the good and the bad of my life and thereby convinced me to live. I went on to earn a bachelor's degree in health education and a master degree in occupational safety and industrial management. I also made key contributions while playing football for Marshall University, and I have devoted most of my life to community service.

I would be remiss if I failed to mention the support that I received from Nick's family, Annie, Chuck, and Amy. They are extraordinary people who treated me as family. Our love and friendship is as strong today as it was over forty-three years ago.

Mr. and Mrs. Marcus Diniaco were also instrumental in my development as a student-athlete. They constantly reminded me that a good education was the most effective way to achieve and enjoy a sustainable life. What's more, they supported me during the good times and the bad times while I was in Huntington and after I departed Huntington. I really appreciate the love that the Diniacos showed me.

Nick Diniaco and Les Hicks

Annie and Nick Diniaco, Chuck and Amy Diniaco

My wife, Delia, Marcus Diniaco, and Les

x

Dr. Marvin Mills Sr., my former college professor, advisor, mentor, friend, and Kappa Alpha Psi fraternity brother urged me to write this book. Therefore, on March 30, 2012, I started this project. Dr. Mills said, "Les, you've never failed or disappointed me, so write your book." I have not disappointed Dr. Mills, who transformed me from an athlete-student to a student-athlete and taught me how to be an accomplished safety professional in the process.

If a picture speaks a thousand words, I have spoken hundreds of thousands because the people cited played a big part in my life.-Marvin "Sticky" Mills

Abe Bryan, the late Steubenville High School head coach

Abe Bryan taught me how to play football and gave me the opportunity to play for Steubenville High's Mighty Big Red. He was an intense competitor who demanded excellence and pushed me to become one of Steubenville High's best defensive ends.

The Mighty Big Red is currently the twenty-second-most winning high school football program in the United States and the third most-winning high school program in Ohio.

September 18, 1923-February 3, 2011
The Coach—Abe Bryan
Big Red's Legendary Coach

What do you say about a coach that comes around once in a lifetime? Born on September 18, 1923, in Steubenville's South End, Coach Bryan was one of 5 children. Coach graduated from Steubenville Catholic Central, and later enlisted in the United States Marine Corps. Coach served in Saipan and Iwo Jima, receiving two Purple Hearts and a Bronze Star.

Shortly after his return to the states, Coach entered Miami University in Oxford, Ohio. During his college days, Coach Bryan and Ara Paraseghian (Notre Dame Coach) became close friends through their interest in football. As roommates, they spent most of their free time talking football and football strategies. After graduating from Miami, and receiving his Master's Degree from the University of Pittsburgh, Coach began a career that would take him to Hall of Fame status.

Beginning in 1951 as an assistant to Coach Ray Hoyman, Coach Bryan would spend the next 13 years preparing for his tenure as the Head Football Coach at Big Red. Coach and his wife Geraldine "Gerry" Oravec Bryan would be blessed with nine children: Becky, Abby, Charlie, Andy, Abe, Jamie, Jeri, Meri, and Robert; 10 grandchildren, and one great-grandchild.

In the spring of 1964, the Steubenville Board of Education made the decision that would change Big Red football forever, as they hired Coach as THE person to LEAD the Big Red Football Program. What a CHOICE ... Winning 59 games in the next 9 seasons would only scratch the surface of how Coach put the BIG back in the Big Red. For the three years following, spanning 65 through 67, the Abe Bryan led Big Red would win 26 of 30 games, enter the All-American Conference, and spend time in each of the 3 seasons as the #1 team in the state. Not in Division II, III, or IV, but the #1 team in the entire state of Ohio. On three different occasions, the Big Red would knock off the #1 team in the state, twice TURNING THE TRICK on Canton McKinley—How do you like that, Coach Nehlen?

Massillon, Canton McKinley, Warren Harding, Niles McKinley, and Alliance would each spend time on the schedule, and in 1970, each of the 5 schools would compete with Big Red as members of the nation's best high school football conference.

Before Coach retired in 1972, he spent time as the President of the Ohio High School Football Coaches Association, and during his tenure, the Ohio playoff system would come to fruition.

Honors have come to Coach Bryan over the years, but as he always told me there is no honor better than leading young men to compete, and let me add, especially if they don the Red & Black.

In closing, the Big Red Football program will always hold a special place for special people, and no one is more special in the hearts of Big Red Football and Big Red Football Fans than Coach Abe Bryan.

We love you, Coach. Watch over us always, and may God bless you always.

Your friend,
Reno

Articles and photos reprinted with permission of Steubenville High School.

"Salty" and Shirley Rogers (Delia's parents) have been phenomenal in-laws who have always been there for us. We appreciate the help and advice you have given us over the years. Salty has always blessed us with a positive outlook on life, and Shirley has been a welcomed addition to our family.

The late Eddie "Rangoon" Simon and I competed for the starting defensive end position in high school. Simon prompted me to bring my A-game to practice every day.

Coach Tom Gardner, one of my favorite coaches, always had my back. He kept me insulated from many trials and tribulations while I was playing high school sports. He was the voice of reason that helped me make intelligent decisions. Coach Gardner's son, "Tom Tom," the basketball team's ball boy, was very polite and hardworking. Coach Gardner and "Tom Tom" will always have special places in my heart.

Mr. Gardner guards and centers

Coach Andy Nameth, my position coach at Marshall, always created an opportunity for me to succeed and had my best interests at heart. I really enjoyed playing for him and regret I was never able to play up to his and my expectations because of injuries and illness. I was unable to attend the premiere of the We Are Marshall movie, but Coach Namath unselfishly gave me the commemorative helmet he received at the event; in his mind, I had earned it.

Seer Shawn R. Williams of Special Forces for Christ Ministries is a brother in the Lord who was another who encouraged me to start this project. He inspired me to fulfill my purpose and potential by instilling in me a "can do" spirit and challenged me to expand my untapped potential. I accepted his and Dr. Mills' challenge to write this book, and I plan to write more.

The late Arthur and Mattie Underwood, the parents of Reggie Oliver, Marshall's quarterback have been an integral part of my life since 1972. They used to bring Reggie, me, and some of our other teammates Vienna sausage, spam, crackers, canned goods, fried chicken, and desserts every home game. Mattie filled the void as my adopted mother; I'm honored she considered me as a son. Arthur and I used to have Sunday conversations about the Herd, the Crimson Tide, Alabama A&M, and the NFL teams for years every Sunday until he passed away. However, we still look forward to talking with Mattie at least twice a week. She imparts wisdom and encouragement to Delia and me.

Al Harris, a highly skilled craftsman at Lockheed Martin encouraged me to write this book. Harris convinced me that this project would motivate and inspire others who are hurting like I had been hurt. I thank Al for getting me off the shore of doubt and into the sea of success.

Coach Don Donatteli was inducted into The Minor Football Hall of Fame. Coach also served in various capacities, assistant principal, principal and school superintendent. He taught me how to play the defensive end position with intelligence and tenacity. While I was in Ohio I visited Toronto High School. Coach was the presiding principal. After my visit with him, he wrote me this letter. I kept this letter for over 26 years. It read.

Donald J. Donatteli, Principal
Toronto High School
Third & Myers Streets
Toronto, Ohio 43964

February 12, 1988

Dear Les,

It was nice to see you. Thanks for taking time to drive up to Toronto High School to say hello.

I want to congratulate you on your fine career and family. I was impressed with your dedication to them and your God. You are such a fine gentleman.

Keep in touch next time you are up this way. We'll have lunch or dinner.

Best to you,
Don Donatteli
Your old coach and you were one of the good ones.

Coach Mike Herrick allowed me to remain on my junior high school basketball team as a manager when I failed to make the team. That painful experience taught me humility. Up to that time in my life, I'd made every team that I'd desired. In addition to that, Coach taught me how to be a team player. We have shared a life-long appreciation and respect for each other.

Coach Jack Lengyel, the legendary head coach of Marshall's Young Thundering Herd, aggressively recruited me, as did Notre Dame, Iowa, Iowa State, California, Minnesota, Ohio State, Syracuse, and many other "blue chip" programs. Coach Lengyel told me, "A lot of teams want you, but we need you." Although I had anticipated being at a major winning football program, I went to Marshall because I embraced the idea of being one of the building blocks that would resurrect the school's football program, not realizing I would end up being a part of history. Coach Lengyel was and still is supportive of his players. Coach Lengyel has served as a friend and confidant over the last forty years.

Reprinted with permission of Coach Jack Lengyel.

This story is about Lester "Les" Hicks, born in extreme poverty in the small, sleepy southern town of Reynolds, Georgia. His parents, George and Clifford Hicks, who were sharecroppers, raised fourteen children in a three-room shack and ingrained in them core values of hard work, honesty, and faith in God.

Lester, an outstanding football player, chose to attend Marshall University after an airplane crash that took the lives of seventy-five people, including its varsity football team, coaches, administrators, staff, boosters, and the plane crew. It was one of the greatest tragedies in college sports history.

Lester, who had been recruited by several top football-playing universities, was told he was needed at Marshall to help re-build its football program, and Lester accepted the challenge.

Throughout difficult times in his early life and his college and professional career, Lester never lost his faith, dedication, commitment, or the hope of succeeding against all odds. While participating in football at Marshall, he learned to treasure each moment; he learned life was very fragile and should never be taken for granted.

Lester is a winner in life because he persevered through all his adversities with a faith in God and his fellow man. He became an accomplished safety engineer and human resources professional at Lockheed Martin, where he has been employed for twenty-eight years. Against all odds, Lester has fulfilled his personal dreams.

Jack Lengyel
Head Football Coach
Marshall University 1970-1974 (retired)

Jack Lengyel had a long and distinguished career in collegiate athletics. He served as assistant football coach at Akron (1969) and Heidelberg College (1963-1965). He was head football and lacrosse coach at the College of Wooster and remained there for four years. However, his greatest task and achievement as a coach occurred between 1971 and 1974, when as head football coach at Marshall University he rebuilt the school's football program after a tragic airline crash killed the team. In 2006, the movie We Are Marshall, released in 2006, told the story of the crash. Matthew McConaughey played the role of Coach Lengyel. Coach Lengyel, involved in athletics since 1957, is an inspirational speaker today.

TABLE OF CONTENTS

This is a great day to be alive! Every great accomplishment starts with the decision, "I'll try!" I apologize in advance for all the feelings I will probably hurt because I did not make public acknowledgement of the countless number of good deeds that poured into my life. My valued supporters include but are not limited to my family members, relatives, friends, teachers, college professors, colleagues, coaches, and acquaintances. To give all of you the honor due to you, I would have a book of acknowledgements only. From the depths of my heart, I thank all of you for making my life better; I'm forever grateful to you.

My faith was and will always be the hope to succeed as it is for most African American families not only in the South but also all over the United States who persevered through countless tribulations. Faith in God provided hope to African Americans when there was seemingly no light at the end of their tunnels, when there was no food in the house, when rent was due, and when they were sick. God is the answer to all prayers. My parents were God-fearing people who taught us to place God at the head of our lives. I can do all things through Christ, who strengthens me. The power of life and death is on our tongue. If you seek first the kingdom of heaven and all its righteousness, God will bless you. By the help of God, I have prevailed against all odds.

CHAPTER ONE

DO NOT DESPISE THE DAY OF HUMBLE BEGINNINGS

BACKGROUND

As you drive down a road defined by a manicured lawn, evenly trimmed hedges, and beautifully aligned hardwood trees, you cannot help but notice a great, white mansion. If you look very closely, you will see an old, run-down shack behind the mansion. This was my home, which sat in front of the landowner's cotton patches, pecan and fruit trees, and soybeans and vegetables entrusted to my family's care in Reynolds, Georgia. Reynolds was a small, sleepy, farming community my parents called home many years before I was born.

During my family's stay in Reynolds, my parents worked for several landowners who demanded that our family, comprising my parents, my fourteen siblings, and four grandchildren, generate a profit, which they thought was the norm. However, my family would ascend from the bowels of despair and hopelessness to experience a somewhat better life in the North.

Our sharecropper shack was held up by concrete blocks sitting on red clay soil and sided with deteriorating wooden boards that, by the grace of God, protected the family from tornadoes, storms, snow, and the scorching Southern sun. The two-bedroom shack had no plumbing, electricity, or bathroom. My parents had one of the bedrooms, and the rest of us occupied the other bedroom.

My parents raised fourteen sons and daughters:

Mattie, "Bay," was a very quiet and easygoing peacemaker and leader who loved the Lord. She migrated to Ohio, where she opened her home to my parents and the rest the family until Dad established himself in Ohio. Everyone spoke highly of Mattie's character. (Deceased)

Mary Evelyn, "Little Sister," is very outspoken. She enjoys cooking, and her sweet potato pies are the best. She's the family historian who possesses a wealth of family history. She gave me a car right before I went to college.

George Jr., "June," was my oldest brother and the family barber. He loved telling jokes and was the life of every party. He worked, though, as hard as he partied. He allowed me to work with him during summer vacations and holidays at a drugstore. Unfortunately, he elected to take his own life by shooting himself through his heart. (Deceased) Odell and George Jr.'s were the proud parents of Geraldine, Darlene, Eugene, Boobie, the late Evelyn, the late Clarence, Rob and Linda.

Catherine passed away when I was fourteen months old. My siblings told me she was a very caring and family-oriented sister. (Deceased)

Willie, "Snook," is a strong-willed man who loves talking politics and telling jokes. I used to spend many summers with him watching sports, playing checkers, and discussing politics. Snook said what he meant and meant what he said. The late Pat and Willie's children are Brian and Leslie.

Darlene, "Doll," was a second mother to me when my mother passed away. I moved into her home shortly after my mother's funeral. I am indebted to Doll and her husband, Jerry Clark, for allowing me to catch my dream. She helped me grow in every conceivable aspect of my life. She was the practical joker in the family. (Deceased)

Ola was always ill. She was a Christian who loved the finer things of life, and she enjoyed singing and dressing up. She used to call me on my birthdays to sing happy birthday to me. She was a strict disciplinarian, but everyone liked her because she had a winning personality. (Deceased) Ola and Walter's children are Tammy, James, Tracy &Terry (twins), Danny, Rodney & Rona (twins).

Charles, "Bubba," was an exceptional basketball player, a natty dresser, and an excellent dancer. He was always there when you needed him. I spent several summers with him and his former wife, Barbara, when they lived in Detroit and Akron, Ohio. Barbara is a very nice person who always treated me like one of her sons. Barbara and Charles are the proud parents of Bobby and the late Anthony. Additionally, Shirley and Charles are the parents of Angel and Jenny.

Charlie James, "Moe," was street tough and feared by many, but he would give you the shirt off his back. He was a ladies' man who had a way with words. He made me tough by using me as his punching bag and tackling dummy. (Deceased) Charlie was the father of Dushawn and James.

Lonnie Bennett, my idol, excelled on the football field as an undersized defensive end. He had an unbelievable work ethic. I wanted to be just like him in sports and work. He was my first sibling who graduated high school. I spent many summer vacations with Lonnie and his wife, Carol, an incredible sister-in law. Carol and Lonnie are the proud parents of Lorena, Laconda, Lavetta and the late Johnna.

Rosetta was very sensitive, kind, and generous person. She always thought I was the greatest; she was one of my biggest fans. Rose never met a stranger and always had a positive outlook about everything. She was family oriented. (Deceased) Rosetta was the mother of Eddie and Shawn.

Roy Lee, my youngest brother, had a lot of ability in the classroom and on the football field and the basketball court. His talents exceeded mine by far. Unlike me, Roy was a charismatic extrovert who could keep the room laughing all the time. (Deceased)

Ann, my youngest sister, is sweet and caring. She loved to talk whenever you got her going. The loss of my parents affected her the most. Ann is a devoted mother to Darryl, Shemeka and Derrick.

My parents also raised four grandchildren:

Ernest, Mary's son, was always very kind and respectful of my parents. He has always been a peacemaker and a very skillful worker with his hands. His wife, Alcenia has meshed into the family seamlessly.

Marion, Catherine's daughter, was always mischievous but had a way of making people like her. She is a practical joker who has learned how to survive.

Clementine, "Clem," Mary's daughter, was very intelligent. She liked adventures and challenges. Clem always got along with everybody in the family. (Deceased)

Shirley, Mary's daughter, had a green thumb. She was very neat and orderly and a good student who enjoyed making people smile. (Deceased)

To paraphrase something my pastor, once said, "Our bedrooms were not large enough to change your mind." I'd share a room with 15 other family members sharing a bed in groups of four. During blazing Georgia summers, a continuous stream of sweat streamed from my forehead, to my ears, under my chin, and all over my chest in a crammed room well over ninety degrees, and we didn't have any fans to help us endure the 24/7 heat. That's what life was like for a sharecropper family in the Deep South.

Moe's loud snore woke me up every night around the same time, making me conscious of the hot, steamy room seventeen of us shared. The odious, overwhelming smells of dirty feet, toe jam, armpits, and gas releases caused me to cover my nose and mouth. Because we slept so close together, I could tell what my brothers or sisters had to eat that day by their farts.

Because we lacked indoor plumbing, we had to find the best spot in the woods to relieve ourselves, but that meant fighting off bees and gnats and avoiding snakes. My parents tasked the older siblings to draw water from the well or the creek to fill five-gallon tubs for bathing. Because we lacked electricity, kerosene lamps provided lighting after dark. Our meat was smoked or cured for preservation and stored in a smokehouse. We didn't have fresh meat or fish unless it had been just slaughtered or caught.

My older siblings would reminisce about what they encountered while playing underneath the house, which was relatively cool. Their rare playtime was interrupted by rattlesnakes and copperheads who were also seeking refuge from the sun. My parents used lime, sulfur and mothballs to drive snakes away.

After torrid summers came bone-freezing, teeth—chattering winters that seeped through countless cracks and crevices in our shack's floor and walls and overpowered our one wood-burning stove. The siblings got a little comfort from snuggling up and nestling closely together, but at times it got so cold in our shack that the devil himself ran around begging for an overcoat.

My family learned to accept the good times and the bad times. My family's survival skills were tested every day; we seldom had a day when there was no chaos. I thank God for parents who loved us and stayed with us in spite of difficult circumstances. They committed their lives to us. Though the meals weren't always appetizing, we always had something to eat for breakfast, lunch, and supper. I cannot recall being hungry while growing up, even though sometimes meals were just syrupy sugar water poured over bread. I commend my parents for making provisions for all of us daily. When you're as poor as we were, you get used to seeing rats, roaches, and flies outside waving "We Will Work For Food" signs. Nonetheless, I wouldn't have changed my parents for any others; I wanted to be just like my dad and marry a woman just like my mother.

Mama and Dad toiled in the field in the shadows of slavery. My father was born in Schley County, Georgia, near the plantation where he'd work. He came from the family of sharecroppers and had only a fourth-grade education. Dad was tall, dark, and handsome. With his six-four, 225-pound frame, he looked like a gladiator. He was very humble, quiet, and peaceful until someone messed with his family.

My mother was a tall, beautiful woman. She had smooth, light-brown skin accentuated by a few freckles on her high cheekbones. She always had an infectious smile with a little twinkle in her eye. She always combed her hair toward the back, except on Sundays, when she'd use a hot comb to make stylish curls.

At age thirty-two, my dad married my mother, who was fourteen. During that era, marriages with such age disparities were acceptable. Although my parents didn't have much education, they were articulate and good at math. Mama went to church every Sunday, but Dad was not as religious as she was because he worked so much. My mother cooked wholesome meals because plowing land and picking cotton, fruits, and nuts was very strenuous work for my dad. She taught all her children how to cook and clean.

My parents moved from plantation to plantation to better our financial and living situations, and some landowners were more sensitive than others toward Negroes.

As I was growing up, I was not aware how difficult life was for my parents, even though my older siblings would remind me of our parents' ongoing struggles. My parents used horses and mules to plow because the landowner didn't buy a tractor until 1953.

Providing an education for Negroes were not a priority for landowners during the 1950s; they wanted their sharecroppers' children to work opposed to going to school. My father never learned to read or write, and my mother had just a sixth-grade education. My siblings, except for Lonnie, didn't have much more than that. Lonnie and I graduated from high school because the family moved north, to Steubenville, Ohio, and were able to take advantage of educational opportunities there. After graduating high school, I earned an associate of arts degree at Ellsworth Community College in Iowa and an undergraduate degree in health education and a graduate degree in occupational safety and industrial management from Marshall University.

I wanted to take full advantage of living in the North. I was blessed because I didn't have to work in the cotton fields when I turned six. Unfortunately, the majority of my older siblings did not have the option Lonnie and I had. They had to leave school in Georgia to work all over the plantation. Sharecropper children weren't paid to study, but actually, they weren't paid for working either; sharecroppers' children labored for free.

The landowner paid my parents $2.50 per week, and cotton was the biggest cash crop. The cotton-picking season ran from October through mid-December. We collected pecans in

November, planted vegetables in the spring, and picked fruit during the summer.

Dad said that D H, one of the wealthiest people in South Georgia, who owned property throughout Georgia and Florida, treated him better than any other landowner had. The D H family married into the A G family, who were slave owners during slavery.

We lived on the DH plantation until D H passed away in 1952, a death that changed our lives forever. H, who respected the work my dad and our family had done for him made Dad his lead farm hand a few years before he passed away. H promised him several acres of land, but after H passed, his widow remarried someone who didn't like the idea of a colored man getting so much land and cheated Dad out of his land, wages, and treated us very harshly. So, my dad found employment with relatives of A G. This turned out to be one of the worst decisions my father ever made. They were not "colored friendly"; they worked our family longer and harder for less money and no respect. If things weren't bad enough, the A G family lived next door to a Ku Klux Klan member. Make no mistake about it—the Klan had always been around, but D H never allowed the Klan to bother our family.

On the other hand, our new landlord allowed the Klan to harass our family more often than not, sometimes every day. The Klan use to beat and spit on Dad and the rest of us. As I saw my family members being abused and oppressed by the landowners and Klansmen, I wanted to get a knife, shovel, rake —anything —to retaliate. During that time in my life, my heart was full of hatred, but I was young and powerless. I reacted by crying more times than I can remember before I was five. I haven't cried more than five times since we left Georgia in 1955. Crying doesn't change things unless you're a baby, and you shouldn't cry over spilled milk. Clean it up or let it dry up and move on!

God requires us to love our enemies, and that's what my parents raised us to do. Observing how badly the landowners and Klansmen were treating us was very hard. By His grace, I allowed God to come into my life. From that day on, I was committed to loving the Devil out of those who were against me or used me spitefully.

After being cheated and abused throughout his life, Dad considered relocating to Steubenville, Ohio. Although I was only four, I liked the idea of moving anywhere outside Georgia. I had overheard or had seen the atrocities my family had to suffer. Oftentimes, I felt like a fat man in quicksand hoping for help; life in the South was that bad.

The move to Ohio was surprising because Dad was not a risk taker. The landowners had brainwashed him into believing that sharecropping was the best livelihood and the ultimate life for us. Everyone in the family thought so, except for my older and more-adventurous siblings, Mattie and Mary. They had their hearts set on going to Atlanta or Steubenville, Ohio.

Leaving South Georgia for Ohio seemed like a great idea to me. I didn't like having to leave school to pick cotton, fruits, nuts, and vegetables, but I didn't have a say in the matter. I never looked forward to being beaten because my free-labor productivity was too low for the tyrannical landowner. I couldn't picture myself with no education, living in a run-down shack that was significantly worse than the landowner's doghouse, and eating the leftover parts of pigs and cows, including the entrails (chitterlings) that landowners considered unfit to eat but was food for our table.

Sharecropper children worked from sunup until sundown without pay. We were blessed if we had two changes of clothes. I remember Mom slicing and dicing chicken neck bones and putting them into a pot with boiling rice. This was a good meal for us. When we were finished with our neck bones, we'd toss them to one of our dogs. "What do you expect me to do with this?" was always the look on our dogs' faces.

Based on all the undesirable things we were leaving behind, I didn't think Ohio would be any worse than Georgia. Mattie, my oldest sister, had been living in Steubenville for several months with no regrets, but I was afraid Dad would change his mind about moving. However, when Mattie's husband, Willie White, showed up at the shack, I knew that against all odds we were moving! Considering what we were leaving behind, it was a no-brainer. Nonetheless, I kept my fingers crossed and prayed without ceasing for this move to take place, and my prayer was answered.

Willie's truck had an open bed, about eight by eight, with eight-foot wooden sides. At the break of a cold, December day, Willie, Junior, and the older siblings loaded one bed, Mama's pots and pans, all our clothes, eleven children (Catherine had passed away, and Mary and Willie had relocated to Atlanta), three grandchildren, and Ola's husband, Junior Gather. Eighteen of us, with all our belongings, minimal as they were, boarded Willie's truck. Willie, my parents, and Ann, an infant, rode in the truck's cab. The rest of us nestled in the back of the truck under homemade blankets for the thirteen-hour journey to Steubenville.

We arrived in Steubenville during the early evening. Several neighbors in the area, which was in the middle of town, had seen us rolling in; they laughed, calling us the black Beverly Hillbillies. To our dismay, we thought we had left our abusive past in Georgia, but this time the abuse was coming from people who looked like us. Satan's spirit of hate and oppression was the common thread that linked Georgia's Ku Klux Klan and some black residents of Steubenville. It matters not whether you're black or white, Satan will inhabit you if you let him. I discovered that black people are prejudice too.

Our first day in Steubenville was one to forget. I began to wonder if Dad had made the right decision. To me, it was like déjà vu all over again. My parents tried to diffuse the neighbors' name-calling and rude remarks. They reminded us that "sticks and stones may break your bones, but names will never hurt you." In reality, the name-calling and verbal abuse really hurt us and led to my older siblings' dropping out of school and fighting almost every day.

Mama knew her kids were fighters. My siblings didn't back down from anybody. My older brothers, George, Willie, Charlie, and Charles were bad to the bone. I can't recall hearing about any of them ever losing a fight. Moe was one of the most feared people in town, and I was a benefactor of their tough-boy reputations; nobody dared put a hand on me because of my older brothers' reputations. Unfortunately, the fear of my older brothers didn't stop the neighbors from mentally harassing my family—they just avoided my older siblings.

Although the neighbors tried to make a spectacle of our family when we arrived, we ignored them because we were tired and weary. Out of the dark, we heard a loud, assertive voice vehemently saying, "Leave those people alone and mind your own business! They aren't bothering you." That was the voice of Ms. Pearl Young. Ms. Pearl gave my parents an extensive orientation to Steubenville. Because Dad was unemployed, Ms. Pearl told him about the welfare system and other important information. Ms. Pearl and Mama became fast friends, close as could be until Mama passed away. Whenever my parents got into a pinch, they could count on Ms. Pearl for anything. I loved Ms. Pearl and her entire family.

After Ms. Pearl interceded on my family's behalf, we climbed out of the truck and went into the house. When we entered the house, even I could see the house was too small. It was time for Dad and Mom to work their magic again, fitting twenty-four people into a house with three bedrooms, a living room, and one bathroom. Mattie, Willie, and her four children slept in their bedroom, while the remaining eighteen of us slept in the other two bedrooms or on the living room floor on padded quilts.

It was a major upgrade, actually. We weren't used to having electricity or plumbing. It took a while to adjust to these amenities that were the norm for the rest of the people in town. This was the first time in my life I could use a bathroom inside a house; I began to feel like the Jeffersons— the Hicks family was moving on up.

We stayed with Mattie, Willie and their children, May Belle, Willie Claude, Leotis, Timmy, and Calvin like sardines in a can for several months. A few years later, my sister gave birth to David and Janie.

The neighbors had judged our family prematurely; they didn't know what was inside my family and me. I refused to believe I was nobody. I used the neighbors' criticisms as a way of finding myself. I've spent my life changing others' perceptions of me in the neighborhood, in the classroom, and on the playing field. Hearing I couldn't do something was always a flame that fueled my desire.

Too often, we allow ourselves to become victims of the lies and criticisms of others, but I have never been one to care what others said about me because I know God. I John 4:4 "Greater is He that is in me that he that is in the world." I Peter 4:8 "God will not withhold any good thing for those who love Him." Psalms 84:11

"Love covers a multitude of sins." As a result, I loved people who were unkind to my family.

Today, I am blessed of the Lord. My blessings have come from treating others the way I wished to be treated. I don't subscribe to "big me—little you" mentality. I realize my life's successes depend on how I treat others. The people you meet going up the ladder are the same people you meet going down it.

SETTLING INTO OUR TEMPORARY HOME

We slept hard that first night until the smell of bacon, eggs, sausage, grits, and biscuits woke everybody up. During the good times we ate like royalty consuming healthy meals with all the trimmings. However, when we fell in hard times we had to take what we could get dining on chicken feet, poke salad, a leafy green plant that grew in the woods, bread and water for several days until Dad could catch a break.

Mama a made soap to clean clothes by boiling water, lye, and other ingredients in a large black kettle that sat on a pile of firewood or coal in the backyard. She allowed the ingredients to cool and solidify. After it solidified, she'd cut it into blocks and wrapped them in wax paper. Mattie didn't own a washing machine, so my mother used large tubs and Cincinnati washboards to clean the clothes. A Cincinnati washboard, made of wood and aluminum, was about twenty-four inches wide and thirty-six inches long. The center of the board had evenly portion ridges on which you'd scrub the clothes. To wring them out, two people stood opposite each other, grabbing the clothes, and twisting them in opposite directions. The clothes were hung on a clothesline strung between two trees or posts and secured with spring-loaded wooden clothespins. This old-fashioned method worked, but it gave the neighbors another reason to laugh at our family, the punch line of every joke in Steubenville after just one week.

Most of the neighbors laughed at our southern dialect. Like E. F. Hutton, when we talked, everybody listened, but for the wrong reasons. They also said we had more people living in our house than the Red Cross could support. The boys had two shirts and two pair of pants, while the girls had two dresses. Our shoes didn't have soles for long stretches. Our bare feet had so much contact with the frozen or sun-kissed ground we thought it was a relative. Dad would secure cardboard and chicken wire under our shoes, but after just a little rain or snow, our feet were back on the ground again.

Why had Dad moved to Ohio during the middle of winter? He must have been very upset with the landowners in Georgia because we weren't prepared at all for the cold northern winters. None of us had winter coats, and it snowed a lot during our first week in Steubenville. My parents had to buy clothes for everyone from the Rescue Mission, which was like a flea market today.

The first time I saw snow, I didn't know if I should play in it or run away from it. I ended up playing with it until my hands froze. I rushed into the house and ran hot water over my hands. That was a huge mistake. I thought my hands were going to explode! I hadn't experienced anything like that in Georgia, and for a brief moment, I longed for Reynolds.

The whole family caught colds and the flu because of the sudden change in the weather. My mother concocted numerous homemade remedies that provided us with pain relief. They were accustomed to making adjustments on the fly in every conceivable aspect of our lives. South Georgia landowners never gave sharecroppers sick time; sharecroppers worked every day unless they were on their deathbeds or giving birth. My younger siblings, Roy and Ann, and I were delivered in a hospital, but my other siblings were born in the shack with the assistance of midwives. My parents did what they had to do, and they were always able to do what was necessary to ensure we were taken care of. We didn't receive care from a doctor; my parents took care of injuries and illnesses with home remedies:

- Common colds and flu—rub Vicks vapor rub on the chest and under the nostrils.
- Mumps— rub sardine-saturated oil under the chin and tie a rag saturated with sardine oil around the chin.
- Nail puncture wounds—place a penny and a piece of salty fatback meat over the wound and secure them with a rag.
- Chicken pox—apply a homemade sulfur salve on the infected areas.
- Cuts—pour sugar in the wound and tie it up with a clean rag. Ear infections—lay your head to the side and pour a capful of peroxide in the ear. Broken bones—snap the bone into place and use wooden slats secured by rags to stabilize the fractured bone. Pink eye—pour a saline mixture into both eyes. Infections — soak any infection in warm Epsom salts. Almost everything else—take a spoonful or two of castor oil.

Looking back, I don't know what my parents would have done without rags, an essential component of their medicine cabinet. My mother's treatment for toothache involved filling a cavity with ground-up aspirin. When a tooth had to come out, she used one of three methods:

- Bite into a hard apple to dislodge the tooth.
- Tie a string around the tooth and yank on the string.
- Place a cotton patch over the tooth and pull it out with pliers.

When the tooth came out, the Tooth Fairy didn't as much as look in the direction of our house because he knew how poor we were.

How MY FAMILY MADE THE TRANSITION FROM GEORGIA TO OHIO

I was four, as I mentioned, when we moved to Ohio. Though we had little more than the clothes on our backs, my parents' decision to move altered the course of my life, though by older brothers and sisters didn't capitalize on the educational opportunities in Ohio.

A MIND IS A TERRIBLE THING TO WASTE

My older siblings, being more sensitive about their tattered clothing, worn-out shoes, and Southern accent didn't like school because their classmates made fun of them, which would get my siblings fighting their oppressors and being sent to the principal's office almost daily. Somehow, Lonnie and I were able to ignore the constant harassment, but our siblings dropped out of school one by one. Although my siblings were not schooled at an early age, they could have done the work. They wasted their opportunities to attain a better education. As was the case with my parents, my siblings were survivors. Most got good-paying jobs in assembly plants, and my older sisters worked as nannies.

DAD LANDS HIS FIRST JOB IN STEUBENVILLE

Dad had to wait until spring to find a job with a construction company because he could lay brick. Though the construction company was in Steubenville, a lot of the work was on the outskirts of town, so my dad had to walk several miles to work, having sold his truck to raise money for our move. He'd get up at 5:00 to be at work at 8:00 every day. I used to watch him soak his feet in warm Epsom salts water to ease his corns and calluses. He used to cut the calluses off with razor blades, a practice that led to his death thirty-nine years later.

In spite of all the hard labor he did, Dad was low-maintenance. He'd have a cup of coffee for breakfast, and Mama would pack a can of Vienna sausages or sardines, saltine crackers, and a moon pie for his lunch. Sometimes he requested baked sweet potatoes. He helped construct many building throughout the Ohio Valley. Whenever I go back home, I feel very proud to know my dad helped build buildings that seemingly will last beyond my lifetime.

In contrast to his physical stature, he was a gentle man — until he was threatened. That's when he became a tower of power. My dad's life was his family, and he sincerely loved Mom. I can't recall Dad raising his voice or a hand to her. He had a certain gleam in his eye whenever Mama was in his presence, and he never allowed his boys to hit their sisters, or any female for that matter.

Our parents taught us to open doors for all women and give gifts from the heart, not just out of tradition, on holidays and birthdays. He liked wearing suits. After cashing his paycheck, he'd dress up just to get out of his work clothes for a few hours, and he would keep his check in his pocket for just a bit before handing his hard-earned money to the bill collector, knowing he'd be broke until the next payday. He'd look pretty dapper in his suit, I remember.

For relaxation, Dad played the guitar, harmonica, and checkers. Outside of my mother, those activities, particularly checkers, made him happy. You could always tell when Dad was on his checker game because he had that signature smile. I loved seeing my father win; that gave him the happiness he deserved. Dad would take on all comers in the house and throughout the neighborhood. He played in houses, on street corners, even in stores, and I'm pleased to say Dad won most of the time.

It was always my dream to earn enough money to buy my parents a big house and let Dad retire; I wanted to provide for them as they had for me. They deserved a rest after raising fourteen children and four grandchildren. Not to question God, but I used to wonder why such good, honest, giving, and devoted parents had to suffer all their lives. They literally worked themselves to death, doing all for their children and grandchildren.

I wanted a good job to try to give my parents a fraction of what they had given me. I was not trying to pay them back for being good parents; I just wanted to show my gratitude to them for devoting their lives to us. However, I didn't know how I could bless them. During that period of my life, I thought college wasn't an option, because no one in my family had ever gone to college. Furthermore, I wasn't aware of any of my neighbors who had attended college. However, my father had two friends, Mr. Hyman and Mr. Luke, who used to talk to me about college, a story I'll tell in a later chapter.

I knew that athletics might be a way to go to college, but, being a product of my environment, I thought I'd end up a steelworker, as did most everyone else in Steubenville. Steelworkers were among the highest-paid workers in the Ohio Valley, and I had hopes of landing a coveted steel-mill job, a good way to buy my parents a big home with many bedrooms, a large kitchen, washer and dryer, and so on, in the nicest neighborhood. I couldn't grow up fast enough to get that mill job.

I remember Dad coming home from work one evening and falling through the floor, breaking his leg and foot. The property owner was never willing to make needed repairs. Not understanding their legal rights, my parents didn't realize they could sue him. Looking back, however, I realize my parents would not have sued him even if they could have because they didn't have that mindset. They were people who didn't want to make a fuss about anything; they were very humble, God-fearing people.

After Dad broke his foot and leg, our income dried up quickly. Ms. Pearl helped my mother submit the paperwork for financial assistance, but it took a few weeks before we received the much-needed financial assistance from the state. The long delay put our family in an "improvise" mode. We ran out of food, and all the utilities were cut off due to lack of payment. Again, my parents had to work some magic. To put food on the table, Dad hunted deer, rabbit, and squirrel. Mama borrowed a little money from Ms. Pearl and bought meal, flour, an assortment of beans, rice, cabbage, white potatoes, and scrap meat parts. Mama ground up the meat with sage, cayenne pepper, and other spices and made the best sausages in town. My parents had the knack to make nothing into something because they knew how to survive.

My mother lived by the philosophy of putting something back for a rainy day, and she certainly did that with her vegetable garden. During the summer, Mama canned tomatoes, corn, green beans, apples, pears, grapes, plums, and peaches to last us through the winter.

When my parents didn't have the money to keep the gas and electricity on, Dad would fire up a black, potbellied, wood-burning stove that would at times turned red with heat. He would place a pot of water on top of the stove to get a little moisture throughout the room, and Mama used the top of the stove for frying meats and boiling vegetables. Because we ate from day to day, we didn't need a refrigerator—there would have been nothing to put in it.

While the water was shutoff, my parents melted snow in five-gallon buckets for cooking and bathing. Even when the house was cold, four people sleeping in one bed kept everyone warmer.

Finally, after a several weeks without any income, my parents received an emergency food order and a check from the State of Ohio Financial Relief System. Emergency food vouchers were good for government cheese, spam, oatmeal, powdered milk, pork and gravy, powdered eggs, raisins, and peanut butter that would put a choke on you. The food came in heavy boxes, and we lived a couple of miles from the warehouse, so my parents bought a red wagon to transport our groceries. This wagon came in very handy for the Sunday paper route Ernest and I handled later.

MY MOTHER

Mama gave birth to a child just about every other year in addition to cooking, cleaning, sewing, and caring for our growing family. Mama always performed miracles throughout my sixteen years with her. I'd watch her transform hopeless moments into exciting adventures. She knew how to mend broken hearts, blankets, and toys. She paid the bills and gave us spiritual guidance and hope. I always stayed close by her side trying to lend a helping hand. I carried groceries, assisted her in the kitchen, and tried to be the best child I could. Mom always cheered me on when I was competing in athletic events.

Just hours before my mother passed away, I had competed in the Bellaire Relays, the biggest track meet in Ohio, from early morning to almost sunset. I came home around 5:30 PM, tired and hungry. I told Mama I'd received ribbons, and she was so proud of me. Placing in the track meet was my Mother's Day gift to her. As an incentive, Mama promised to buy me a typewriter and to bake my favorite cake, pineapple with caramel icing.

That night, Mama had prepared fried chicken, collard greens, rice, cornbread, banana pudding, sweet potato pie, and lemonade. It had been a beautiful day, until approximately 8:30 PM. My niece Marion slapped me on my head, and I hit her back. Mama chastised me for hitting Marion, and that made me angry; I thought she'd showed favoritism toward Marion. Things, however, settled down, and Mama, as she was accustomed to doing, made sure her kitchen was clean and the rest of the house was tidy. She ironed that night for ten in the house, including herself, for mandatory Sunday church services, and she made sure everybody rehearsed Mother's Day speeches.

By 11:30 PM, Dad, five siblings, and four grandchildren had gone to bed. I stayed up to watch Chiller Theater, a horror show hosted by Boris Karloff, on our one TV in my parents' bedroom, until 1:00 AM and went to bed.

At 1:21 AM, Dad woke me. He was visibly saddened. "Call your sister. Your mother's sick." I got out of bed hurriedly and went to her room. Mama's eyes were open. Even as a sixteen-year-old, I knew something was not right. Mama was gone. I trembled as Dad stood beside me. I felt his pain and sadness. I knew this unthinkable loss would affect us all for the rest of most of our lives. I called my sister, Doll, who lived about ten minutes away. It was very difficult for me to speak the words of reality, "Mama's gone."

News of Mama's death traveled like wildfire. Even during a terrible storm that came up that night, well-wishers came pouring into our house even after 3:00 AM. Most everybody loved my mother, who had never met a stranger or refused to feed the homeless. This God-fearing woman always prayed for the sick.

I vividly and painfully remember the undertakers coming for Mama and carrying her out as though her body had no value. I was furious about that for a long time, until I received a heart of forgiveness from our Lord and Savior.

It took me years to forgive myself for not telling Mama I was sorry for hitting Marion, for not telling her good night that night, for not telling her I loved her. My failure to say that last good-bye to Mama provided me with the anger required to play football. I played every sport with a chip on my shoulder due to that anger and sorrow.

MY MOTHER'S HOME GOING

As expressions of love for Mama, many mourners came with food, cards, flowers, and money. Dad was in incredible pain. He and Mom had raised us, moved to Ohio, and lived Christian lives in our presence. In the form of a heart attack, death took Mama away from us when she was fifty-four. I didn't want to attend Mama's funeral for a few reasons, including guilt, denial, and witnessing Dad's pain. I didn't want the last memory of my mother to be of her in a casket, but the rest of my siblings and Dad made me attend her home going.

The church was large enough to hold most who came to Mama's home going, and some stood outside the church to see her casket. On May 10, 1967, Mama was buried in Union Cemetery. I had lost my inspiration to succeed in life on Mother's Day. She had been my friend, comforter, and protector. She taught me to love everyone in spite of racial or cultural differences.

I recall when my parents relocated from our house on South 6th Street to Market Street. The Hood family—Georgianna, Linda, Harry, Richard, Bill, Gabby, and Audrey—a white family, lived next door. They had much less than what we had; they didn't own a TV, and they ran out of food frequently. Being Christians, my parents invited the Hoods over every evening and fed them first, and then gave them the best seats in the house so they could watch TV. This was the routine for almost two years. My parents treated them as family, and the Hoods reciprocated. My parents taught us by the Word and by example that we should love people regardless of their color.

LIFE AFTER MAMA'S DEATH

Life after my mother's death was very hard for me. Except for my older sister who passed away when I was a little over one, I hadn't experienced death in my family, and Mama's death had been so fast on what had seemed to be a typical Sunday morning.

From that day on, the sun didn't shine as brightly, the birds didn't chirp as bountifully, and my problem-solving abilities didn't come as easily. I didn't know how to react to the death of a loved one, especially my mother. Although Dad was the breadwinner, Mama had been the glue that had held the family together. Most important, my mother motivated us to succeed in school. I promised my mother I would graduate grammar, middle, and high school.

I'd give anything to have an opportunity to tell my mother I loved her just once more. I had a very difficult time forgiving myself for over thirty-two years for not having done so until I allowed God come into my life and repented for all my sins.

How MY MOTHER'S DEATH AFFECTED DAD

Mama's passing made Dad's eyes flicker. His once-proud shoulders sunk, and his smiles became noticeably absent. He didn't shave or dress up; he just sat around, playing his harmonica and guitar in a dark room. He had lost his best friend, even if she was still there in spirit. Dad recovered over time somewhat and started cooking, providing the rest of us with encouragement, and the will to survive.

I could sense Mama cheering me on. In fact, I lost my fear of dead people when Mama passed. I knew she would protect me from the rest of the dead people. When I sin, the Holy Spirit and Mama serve as my conscience. I find myself repenting for all my wrongdoings and praying every morning and night. I thank God for protecting me even though I had turned my back on Him. Although I'm almost sixty-two, I'm still mindful of my childhood teachings. I thank God my parents didn't spare the rod; their chastisement made me a contributor to society. My parents were not my pals or best friends; they made it perfectly clear who the parents were and who the children were in our house. We didn't try to meet them halfway on issues, we didn't talk back, and we didn't slam doors. Any outbursts led to serious whippings. Some parents try to be their children's best friends instead of parents, and the children lose respect for them. George and Clifford Hicks taught us their rules:

Thou shall not talk back: It was unthinkable for a child to talk back to parents during the '50s, '60s, and early '70s. Back then, my parents would give us a certain look that would strike fear into our hearts and let us know we were headed for a spanking. That entailed finding five or six young branches in the backyard that Mama would braid into a tight spiral. Mama or Dad would bend the "spankee" over her or his lap or have the victim lie across a bed. The child being spanked would cry for mercy.

After a spanking or two, I would change my ways. I remember my last spanking; I was five, and I tried faking a heart attack because Mama was spanking me so hard. I cried out, "My heart's bursting." Mama, being full of wisdom, said, "I'm going to beat that Devil out of you and then call the pastor. We'll pray for you." My old-school parents were firm believers in not sparing the rod at the expense of spoiling the child, but it usually took only a certain look to get us all to behave.

Thou shall always respect the elderly: My parents taught us to respect elderly people always — open doors for them, carry their groceries, shovel their snow, run their errands, offer our seats to them, and give whatever assistance they needed. In addition, we were required to address older people with "Yes Ma'am," "No Ma'am," "Yes Sir," and so on.

Thou shall not abuse women: My parents did not condone their sons mentally or physically abusing their daughters. It did not matter if our sisters instigated the confrontation or not, we boys had to grin and bear it or face serious consequences.

Thou shall make up the bed when you get out of it: We had to make our beds as soon as we got up. Mama said that people who stayed in bed all morning were more prone to laziness.

Thou shall not leave dirty dishes in the kitchen sink: Our kitchen was clean all the time. Mama was a strict enforcer of the clean-as-you-go philosophy; she didn't like dirty dishes about while she was cooking; that was unsanitary in her mind.

Thou shall not steal: My parents taught us to work for everything we got, and they led by example. They never took anything that didn't belong to them. They taught us to give employers an honest day's work for an honest day's pay. Looking back, I have to apologize for taking apples, cherries, pears, and tomatoes off the neighbor's trees and from their gardens — Mama would have given me a serious beat-down had she known of my transgressions.

Thou shall not go to the community swimming pool: The local swimming pool was off-limits to all of us because two kids had drowned there. Besides, no one in my family knew how to swim.

Thou shall not go to the pool hall: Because some people had been killed in the pool hall, it was off-limits for us. Mama told us she didn't like the idea of her children being around smokers and gamblers, and, as you'll later read, her words were prophetic.

Thou shall not miss church services: Mama required all children living at home to attend church on Wednesdays and Fridays and twice on Sundays. If we missed church, we weren't allowed to play with our friends. We didn't miss many church services.

These were just a few of the significant rules my parents required us to follow while staying under their roof.

MY FIRST JOBS

My nephew Ernest and I landed a job delivering the Pittsburgh Post-Gazette, Enquirer, the Cleveland Plain Dealer, and other popular newspaper and tabloids on Sundays. We had seventy-five customers all over the city. Although we were both young, we appreciated all the pretty girls who lived at some of the houses we delivered to, and I looked forward to those Sunday deliveries. We were like the Pony Express; we delivered the Sunday newspapers rain, sleet, or snow, and we always returned in one piece. Our route concluded at the top of a hill, and we'd ride the wagon my parents had bought at a speed of approximately thirty-five miles per hour with no brakes. We had to cross seven streets before coasting to a stop at the bottom of the hill. That we never got hurt was a miracle. We know we were blessed of the Lord.

My brother Lonnie, my nephew Ernest, and I worked for our pastor, Reverend Livingston, who hauled garbage from residences and stores. We were paid anywhere from $1 to $2 per day and got chocolate milk, cinnamon rolls, and on a good day a bologna sandwich for lunch. On many occasions, he gave us out-of-date candy, overripe fruits, and pastries. He used to give boxes of goods to a poor family with seven kids.

We worked the garbage route every day for about three years, except for one day. I can't remember why we couldn't work for the reverend that day. A four year old boy was killed when the reverend accidently ran over him while backing up; the reverend's spotter lost sight of the child, who was trying to grab an apple that had rolled under the truck. Lonnie, Ernest, and I are still troubled by the death of this child. We wonder if our presence would have made a difference. However, if you believe in destiny, destiny says no. Every man, woman, or child has an appointment with death. As for the reverend, he became ill. I believe he grieved himself to death because he died a few months after the tragic accident.

I worked seasonal jobs, shoveling snow, raking leaves, shining shoes, helping grocery shoppers, and caddying at the Steubenville Country Club. During that early 1960s, 99 percent of the golfers were white, but they paid the caddies decently because most were rich.

Mr. Joe Horston was one of the few black golfers in Steubenville, and he was one of the best golfers, if not the best. He was always nattily dressed; his outfits matched to a T on and off the golf course, and he wore a hat or cap all the time. He was one of the most respected men in Steubenville and was one of the most feared at six-four and 260 pounds. He was very wise and all business.

Mr. Horston was instrumental in finding jobs for the youth during summers. I jumped at the opportunities he set before me to take some of the financial load off my parents. I bought clothes, tennis shoes, and pastries. When I was young, I'd visit the bakery two or three times a day if my money was right. I was on a first-name basis with all the bakery employees, and Ms. Dellalis, one of the older employees, took a liking to me. When she saw me approaching the bakery, she'd fill two bags with donuts and pastries for me for free or for fifteen cents; the cost was based on how near the owner was to the sales floor. I tried to make sure the owner was way out of sight, of course. I frequented all the bakeries in the city and was blessed by many bakery employees. After leaving the bakery, my next stop was any store that sold chocolate milk. That's how I treated myself.

On one occasion, when I earned a considerable amount of cash, I purchased my own tennis shoes. High-topped Chuck Taylors were everybody's choice in the late 1950s. They came in black or white and sold for about $3.99. To be in with the fellas, you had to have them. Another brand, US Keds sold for about $1.99 a pair. If I didn't have enough money to buy my own tennis shoes, I received hand me downs. Unfortunately, after a couple brothers had worn them, they would be in bad shape. When I got them, the labels on the US Keds read "Kush" because they were that worn out, making me the punch line of almost every joke around town when I'd wear them. Our family was the Rodney Dangerfield of the city—we got no respect because of our Southern accent, raggedy clothes, and haircuts. We constantly had to fight for respect.

We feuded with two menacing families who lived in the neighborhood, but there were times when our families got along. We'd play together and share treats. Unfortunately, peacetime was always short lived because those families didn't respect us, and the least little thing would start us feuding again.

My first and best friend in Steubenville was Teddy Freeman. He and I forged a friendship that lasted until his death. He and I were inseparable, and most people thought we were brothers; he and I were together from sunrise to sunset. We went from cowboys to girls and along the way endured hard times and good times.

When we were young, Teddy and I worked an assortment of jobs in order to earn money. As we grew older, we earned or lost money by pitching pennies, nickels, dimes, and quarters. We also played blackjack and tonk, a card game blacks played for money. Tonk players could win if their five cards totaled forty-nine or fifty right off the deal, but that was rare. They could also win by getting three to four cards of the same suit or getting the lowest hand. Tonk, popular fifty years ago, is still going strong. Teddy was a very good pool player, but Mama didn't let me play, but I backed Teddy, and we won more than we lost.

Teddy became an All-State basketball player. I chose football because I loved the physical contact. Teddy and I played on the high school basketball team, but it wasn't my passion, so I was generally the first big man off the bench. Our high school basketball team was a semifinalist in Ohio with a 23-1 record in 1969, which got our team a top-ten rating.

We saw a dead body when we were nine. As we were playing on a hot summer day, we smelled a foul odor coming from an old, vacant house. We walked in, and the smell got stronger. We found the body of an older man, a drunk, in the back room. His body had swollen and burst, and bodily fluids were all over the room. Teddy and I also saw two drunks who had been run over by a train. They were horribly mutilated. These deaths, seemingly all around us, had a lingering emotional effect on us.

Teddy said he'd not want to die in a car wreck or by drowning. It was never determined how Teddy died. His body was recovered in the Ohio River on a frigid-cold January day south of Steubenville. I disclosed I didn't want to die in a fire or drowning. In spite of being members of families who were struggling financially, aside from all of the things that we could not control, we enjoyed growing up and having all kinds of conversations. Teddy and I would often have very deep discussions regarding life, jobs, family, and death. Both of us wanted to get a good mill job, buy a car, rent a house, and live happily ever after. Teddy dreamed about being a doctor or firefighter, while I dreamed about being an astronaut, preacher, or police officer. In fact, we worked on the police force as police cadets during summer vacations.

The Young, Freeman, and Jackson families were the first families to welcome us to Steubenville, and they've been our friends since 1955.

The Young family consisting of Ms. Pearl, Ida Mae, Pooh, Teresa, Frances, Bobby, and Bernadine, tried to make our transition to Steubenville easier. She showed my mother around town and provided our family with financial support. Ms. Pearl and my mother became fast friends, and some people mistook them for sisters.

The Freeman family, consisting of James, Betty Sue, Raymond, Jean, Wayne, Ozella, Nathanial, Lavert, Teddy and Ronnie, hit it off with my family immediately. Their children paired up and hung out with us, and our families are still closely knit.

The Jackson family, Edward, Pamela, Tino, Phyllis, and Dianne, were very good people as well. They helped us in many ways, and George and my dad forged a lasting friendship. For a while, Tino used to terrorize my nephew Ernest and my sister Rosetta. He also chased them with his bulldog, Peanuts, until Moe intervened. Then, peace was restored, and from that point on, my brother, sister, and Tino were the best of friends. Tino served as my sister's bodyguard until she passed away.

Tino didn't harass me probably because I was much younger than my older siblings; he knew Moe didn't allow anyone to bully me. Tino would give me snacks all the time, and he gave me a Lionel train set when I was six, and I kept it for years.

Tino, my brothers, and Rosetta assumed the roles of my personal protectors. They would not let anyone or anything harm me, but I still feared ghosts.

I SAW DEAD PEOPLE

I used to have nightmares about dead people, and I think they started when I was about four. I would listen to my older siblings' ghost stories, including the "Chasing Lady": Once upon a time, a husband caught his wife cheating with another man. He reacted by cutting off her head in the gangway of the house where we were living. As the story went, every rainy night the headless woman would wander our street looking for our gangway to find her head, tormenting anyone who got in her way. I always tried to be in the house before it got dark, especially on rainy nights. On occasion, Mama would ask me to go to the store, and I couldn't say no even though I'd be worried about the Chasing Lady. I'd ask a sibling to go with me, but they would say no. I went to the store very reluctantly, and the trip was more frightening because there was a funeral home on my street. I had to pass the funeral home prior to reaching the store. There was no other way to get to the store. I'd get a running start, close my eyes, and race past the funeral home, cars or no cars. Coming back was a problem because I'd be carrying groceries, which would slow me down as I ran past the funeral home. I had to run down my gangway, about thirty yards long, and manage the eighteen steps into the house before I felt safe. I repeated this agonizing process for twelve years. The fear of the Chasing Lady ended when Mama passed away. I'd tell you how I overcame this fear in an upcoming chapter.

I didn't like attending funerals because of the nightmares they would cause; I'd dream of the dead person in the casket for many nights following a viewing, and that was when I was unable to get to sleep at all. I also used to suffer from a phobia called the "Riding Witch." I'd been told that a witch was riding me whenever I was sleeping, and I would feel as though I were being smothered. I wanted to cry out but couldn't because I was paralyzed. That happened to me at times until about fourteen years ago.

CHAPTER THREE

HOW I DEVELOPED MY FOOTBALL SKILLS AND MADE FRIENDS

PHYSICALLY AND MENTALLY TOUGH

Being the twelfth of fourteen children, I had to be physically and mentally tough to handle all the teasing and slapping coming from my older brothers and sisters, who would use me as their punching bag. When Mama wasn't around, they made me do their chores, including shoveling snow, raking leaves, and fetching buckets of wood and coal. Moreover, they made me make grocery-store runs for them during inclement weather.

FAMILY FRIENDS IN OHIO

After making friends with Teddy Freeman, I forged a friendship with the Gray family, which included Marshall, the late Arthur, Gay, Deborah, and Van, currently known as Rashid Alsabur. The Grays lived right across the street from us, and the Gray brothers and I played on the same football team. They were very good football players, and we were like family. Marshall married his childhood sweetheart, Leona.

The Livingston family: Ron, Brian, Debbie, and Cynthia lived three houses down. Their grandfather became my family's pastor. We use to make racing carts, but never remembered about brakes, until we were at the bottom of the hill. We used to play King of the Hill, jump rope, and Red Light Green Light, which called for everyone but the "caller" to line up and wait for the caller to yell "Green light!" That's when we'd run until the caller would yell, "Red light!" All the runners would have to stop immediately, and anyone who wobbled a bit was disqualified. The game kept you on your toes.

The Walton family: I met Charles "Frog", Christie, Connie, and Gail and their parents, Charlie and Frances at church. "Frog," didn't play organized football because he was undersized, but that didn't stop him from playing the game. He was a good football player and a better friend. He'd run interference for me when I was attempting to date Pastor Thompson's daughter, Donna. Pastor Thompson was against teenage dating, so we'd have to devise plans that allowed me to see her. That was only twice a week because she lived about two hours away.

The Watkins family: I knew the late Richard, Bobby, Patricia, Peggy, Roland, Pam and their parents. When Richard and I weren't playing together on the South End football team, we'd play electric football, basketball, and hockey games with Dwight Platt. Richard and I used to go trick or treating together, and back then, we'd do it for seven days. We loved the candy bars and hated the apples, of course.

The Horston family: The late Mr. and Mrs. Joe Horston, Reynard, the late Sadie, the late Joe Jr., Buster, the late Zachery, the late Stephanie, and Robin accepted our family with open arms. Buster and Moe became very close friends. Moe, Buster, and some other friends were hanging out the night Buster was struck by a truck that tragically ended his life on Route 7. Reynard, a lifelong friend is married to his devoted wife, Debbie.

The Church Family: William Sr. and Laura, William "Sonny" Jr., Joan, Tom "Man", Louis and their parents lived behind us. They provided our family with help when needed.

The West/Williams Family: The late Mrs. Annie Ruth and Mr. West, Sonny, Charlene, Dollie, Louise, Jock and Sister were also a family that I held in high regard including Dollie's husband, Steve.

The Platt family: I also developed speed by circumstances I wouldn't recommend. Dwight Piatt's parents bought him everything, including those electric sports games I mentioned, so Dwight had many friends. However, there was a price to pay for being Dwight's friend. He was an unwilling loser, who'd pull out his pellet gun or his father's gun and threaten to shoot us when he lost a game. He'd chase us out of his house, into the woods, and across streams. We were just ten and didn't sense any danger. In a crazy way, we liked being chased by someone who could have taken our lives. We flirted with Dwight's death sentences for over two years because we weren't worried about dying. In fact, we thought we were going to live to be old men. In retrospect, I realized that God spared my life because he had purpose for me.

Because being Dwight's friend was too risky, I forged relationships with Tommy West and Sammy Willis. Sammy was my first Caucasian friend. The three of us would hang out in the woods, chasing and catching snakes. We caught several snakes every summer, and that's when we'd also raid fruit trees and gardens. I remember climbing up a cherry tree to fill my pockets with the fruit. When I saw the owner's dog, I jumped out of the tree and started running with both hands in my pockets because I didn't want to lose any cherries. But by doing so, I lost my speed, and a black and white Dalmatian bit me through my jeans and pierced my butt. I fought him off with a stick lying in the yard.

I ate the cherries hurriedly because I didn't want Mama to know I'd been "borrowing" anyone's cherries. When I ran into the house, my butt was bleeding. When Mama asked what had happened, I told her a wild dog had bitten me. My mother paid someone to take me to the emergency room, about two miles away, where a doctor gave me a tetanus shot. Unfortunately, for me, my troubles didn't end there. Mama gave me a spanking for getting my new jeans ripped. Though I went on to raid fruit trees every summer, no dog ever caught me again.

The Palmer family: Jeff, Mark, and I became friends after we had a fight about something I can't recall. We were in the fourth grade, and our friendship endured on and off the football field. He and I competed against each other in midget football and Little League. We were high school teammates. Mark's dad, the late Mr. Denny Palmer, was assistant superintendent of the Steubenville public schools. Being around Mark's dad was a good thing — he was a successful African American who was highly respected throughout Steubenville. Mark has been happily married to Vanessa for over forty-two years.

During the winter a few of my friends, Teddy Freeman, John Saxon, the late Charles Prentice, the late Jeff Dawson, Henry Hill, Glenn Hill, Craig Hill, Bill Brooks, Rick Johnson, Tee Thomas, Wayne Brooks, Bobby and Bobby Barker, James "Bugs" King, Jerry Crawford, Nardie Smith, Newt Smith, Keith Dorsey, Larry Brown, Howard "Pumpkin" Birden, Tommy Turner, my brother, Roy plus other younger guys; Billy Zimmerman, Craig Dawson, Dudley Prentice, Amos Johnson, Davey Barker, Dooney Simon and I would clear snow and ice off the playground to play basketball or football. To make it interesting, we'd play for money, from ten cents to a dollar per game. That kind of money made the games very competitive and intense, and we'd play for hours. Afterward, we'd go home and run hot water over our frozen hands. That was a very bad idea once again; I can still feel the pain.

During summers, we'd play touch football in the street until someone tackled an opponent instead of touching him. That's when touch football became tackle football, even on the street. Oftentimes, I'd be tackled and bang into parked cars, fire hydrants, and curbs and end up with skinned elbows and knees and scrapes on my hips.

Two older kids, Bill Hawkins and the late Tommy Reed, arranged our neighborhood football team. I lived on the south side of town, but we played all across the city on vacant lots, ball fields, school playgrounds, grassy areas along Route 7, in front of libraries, and on hospital lawns. Although I was tall and lanky, I was a good running back who enjoyed running over would-be tacklers. The late Coach Reed dubbed me The Les Machine because I never stopped running.

I recall one game on a library lawn. I was running the ball along the left sideline when someone tackled me. I hit the ground, and my head slid into a sharp metal link at the base of a fence and cut me about half an inch behind my left ear with a sound like a beverage can opening. I knew I was hurt badly; my teammates said they could see the white meat inside my head. However, I didn't want to stop playing because we were losing. I found a napkin, which I rolled up and stuck into the hole behind my ear, and played the rest of the game. Back at home, I received additional treatment from my mother.

During another game, I was tackled on a concrete crosswalk in a schoolyard. I fell on my face, and that led to three teeth coming through my lower lip.

THE SOUTH END FOOTBALL TEAM

I will always be grateful for the time the late Tommy Reed and Bill Hawkins had a vision for the South End football team. Those two took many young, hopeful football players like me off the streets, libraries, schoolyards, and other grassy areas to places more suitable for football. They taught me the fundamentals of tackling, blocking, running, and catching. Coach Reed and Coach Hawkins took time to care about all the young boys living on the south side. They scheduled games with older, bigger, and faster boys and encouraged me and others to strive for perfection through hard work. I took a great deal of pride in being the hardest worker on the team and later on the job.

MY TRANSITION TO AN ORGANIZED FOOTBALL LEAGUE

After Coach Reed and Coach Hawkins jump-started my budding football talents, I signed up for the Youth Football League. That required players to be drafted by one of the teams and then selling thin mints to buy equipment and uniforms. Our division comprised of twelve teams, and ours came in first or second every year. I was the starting wide receiver and starting defensive end. After a successful showing in the Youth Football League, I was ready for the Grant School Junior High team, but Mama was afraid of the physical contact, and she had her reasons.

I recall playing left field in a baseball game. I lost track of my surroundings while trying to catch a fly ball and ran full-speed into a flagpole, fracturing my jaw. My face and chest were covered in blood, and my jaw began to swell. I ran home, which was across the street. My mother didn't like the sight of blood. She cried, "Jesus, help my child!" and ran down the back steps. After the rest of the family calmed her down, they took me to the hospital for what turned out to be three fractures of my jaw and a lacerated chin that required four stitches. The doctor secured my jaw, so I went on a liquid diet—soups, mashed potatoes, sweet potatoes, oatmeal, and grits—for six weeks. Those six weeks seemed like six years.

EARNING A SPOT ON THE GRANT
SCHOOL JUNIOR HIGH TEAM

After I recuperated from my broken jaw, I asked my mother if I could try out for the middle school football team. Mama said no repeatedly; she was afraid I might get hurt by one of the hard-hitting bigger boys. I finally wore her down, however, and started preparing myself to play.

When I finally convinced Mama I could handle the physical contact, I tried out and earned a spot on the team even though I was recovering from the broken jaw and had lost a lot of weight due to my restricted diet. I saw stars every time I made contact with another player, but I played through the pain and made the starting lineup my first year at Grant. My mother, however, refused to watch me play; she just couldn't bear to see me hit by bigger boys.

It was an honor to earn a spot on the team, a perennial power in the Ohio Valley. The Grant Tigers always played freshman and junior varsity teams in Ohio and West Virginia because we were that good and we knew it. Because of my hard work, I earned a backup defensive end position as a seventh grader and a starting position as an eighth grader. After I graduated from Grant Junior High, I was ready to fulfill my lifelong dream of playing for Steubenville High School's Mighty Big Red.

Regarding my mental toughness, my new neighbors abused me. They said that I wouldn't make it because I was a poor Southerner whose parents had minimal resources. The neighborhood kids laughed at me because I was quiet and shy and didn't have decent shoes. I ignored all the locker-room jokes about me and stayed on the team because I loved to compete. I learned to be tough skinned and ignore negative remarks about my family and me. I refused to let anyone deter me from reaching my goal. My pastor and parents taught us we could do all things through Christ, who strengthens us. I know God rewards those who diligently seek Him.

How I DEVELOPED STRENGTH

My parents could not afford to buy weights, and I didn't have access to a weight training room, but my brother Lonnie taught me to improvise. Lonnie, my only sibling who started on the high school football team, had an outstanding work ethic. We lived beside a metal salvage yard where he collected what we needed for weight training, all kinds of iron parts and even a car axle. To make his forearms hard, he'd hit them against a smooth brick wall at least a hundred times every day. I closely observed Lonnie and did everything he did and more; over time, I improved my strength significantly. I used these homemade weights until I had access to the high school facilities and the YMCA.

In the late '50s and throughout the '60s, there were no PlayStations, Nintendos, or other games that produce couch potatoes. Back in the day, we played hopscotch, jump rope, and all kinds of racing games, and that's how I developed the speed I needed to play football successfully.

CHAPTER FOUR

PLAYING FOOTBALL AT
STEUBENVILLE HIGH SCHOOL

A LIFELONG DREAM FULFILLED

When I was in grammar school and junior high, I'd scale a big chain link fence topped with barbed wire to sneak into Steubenville's Friday night football games. Because we were the Mighty Big Red, one of Ohio's perennial powers, no one doubted the outcome. The highlight of my evening was climbing over the guardrails and on to the playing field after the game. I remember running all over the field and tackling make-believe future stars.

Steubenville High's field was immaculate. Old Big Red (our mascot stallion) logo and the Steubenville High logo were painted in the end zones. The word around Ohio was that Steubenville's playing field was second only to Ohio State University's field.

I really felt good about being on the team, and I was getting some playing time. Most important, my mother was not as paranoid as before about my getting hurt. In addition, most of my teammates were beginning to accept the outcast from South Georgia. But where there's good, evil is always present. Suddenly, like a thief in the night, death took my mother. For the first time in my life, I had nowhere to turn for comfort. My guardian angel was gone. During that time, anger and frustration build up inside me, and I took it out in sports. When I thought about the passing of my mother, my quiet, mild-mannered demeanor became aggressive; I had the desire to inflict pain on anyone in my way. I recall hitting opponents and teammates so hard that I saw stars. I was a man possessed and tried to play that way. I didn't feel pain; I just wanted to inflict it. The chip on my shoulder during all athletic competition was due to the fact I had lost her too soon and that she would never see me play.

When I stepped onto the field as a member of the freshman team, the electricity was overpowering. Everyone was blocking, tackling, and catching passes all over the practice field, like an NFL Today promo to game time. There was no way I was going to relinquish my dream. My coaches began to sing praises about my play, and I can still hear their voices. It was downright intoxicating—I was on a roll and practicing confidently and at a high level. I began to make a name for myself.

In addition, I developed social skills; I was interacting with the other players on and off the field more, and my play on the football field caused me to perform better in class. I hoped that the rest of my life would get better as well after having experienced a tough life in Georgia and Ohio. I worked out all the time. Failure was not an option.

FRESHMAN FOOTBALL

I feverishly prepared for the upcoming freshman football try outs. My mother's death put me in a state of depression for several months, but Teddy Freeman and my brothers Moe, Charles, Lonnie, and Willie convinced me to participate in the summer practices. I could not accept the fact that my mother was gone, but I gradually made mental adjustments and attempted to move on.

The coaching staff asked me to play receiver and defensive end. The defensive end position was tough because we had an outstanding group of running backs, including Reynard Horston,

Tim Williams, Mark Palmer, Larry Brown, Tom Mitchell, and the late Raymond Culbreath. The fullback was the late Scottie Robinson. Our running backs tried to follow in the footsteps of former high school greats such as Harry Wilson, Leon and Herbie Lindsey, Keith Burke, Michael Palmer, Raymond Terry, Don Osby, Oonie Sims, and Bob Smith. Reynard's late brother Zack was an excellent fullback.

As a defensive end, I had to have my A-game on every practice to contain Reynard and Raymond, and I held my own. Practicing against athletes with extraordinary talent made me better. I was a starter because I dedicated that season to my mother.

THE SOPHOMORE SEASON

At Steubenville High, the competition got more intense as you approached the varsity squad. The Big Red football program didn't have to rebuild when seniors graduated; it simply reloaded from a large talent pool every year. Our freshman and junior varsity teams played a level or two higher than their classes. I enjoyed a solid season on my way to varsity.

MY FIRST YEAR ON VARSITY

My football career was going swimmingly until my junior year. The team and I had a year not to remember. Our bubble burst; the team uncharacteristically went 4-6 due to many injuries at key positions, player dismissals, and some players quitting the team. I didn't do anything different from the previous years, but I just didn't get the playing time. My position coach thought the seniors were better than I was, and he judged me against my brother Lonnie. He said that Lonnie was a hardnosed over achiever and wanted me to be more like Lonnie. This was the lowest point in my high school playing career; I was just a spectator. However, I was motivated and couldn't wait for the next season. I started preparing right after the last game of my junior season.

SENIOR YEAR—DO OR DIE

After my disastrous junior year, I had to determine why I had failed to get playing time. I was six-four and 174 pounds without muscles to speak of; too small to play defensive end even by high school standards. I didn't weigh more than two dead flies. I sold thin mints to earn my membership at the YMCA facilities, where I used the gym and the weight room. That's where I met Officer Leon Stinson of the Steubenville Police Department, who lifted weights for prize money. I asked him to work with me, and he agreed. He worked me very hard, and I began to see my body filling out with muscle. I was lifting more weight than I had ever imagined. I used spring-loaded handgrips at every opportunity to help me control offensive players. I banged my forearms against brick walls 250 times daily to make them hard as brick for when I'd hit blockers' helmets and shoulder pads. My height and long arms gave me an advantage over offensive players. My teammates called me "Golden Forearms" and "Excedrin Headache Number 84" because I hit that hard.

I ran in the gym because it was too cold to run outside, but I would run until I was exhausted, with barely enough energy for the long miles home. That's how I got bigger and stronger by spring, the start of practice. I had adequately prepared for the weight training sessions, and the coaching staff acknowledged my weight gain and increased lifting capacity. In addition to being faster and stronger, I was way ahead of where I had been the previous year, and my hard work caught the coaches' eyes.

During the summer, I got a job in the Weirton Steel Mill, working 7:00 AM-3:00 PM, 3:00 PM-11:00 PM, and 11:00 PM-7:00 AM shifts. I didn't mind the hours or the job assignments; I was happy to be working and taking home more than $500 a week, a lot of money even for a parent back then.

I was looking at the calendar every day to see how close I was to the August 15 start of football practice, and I was training even harder, liftingweights and running seven days a week. Because of my work schedule and because some of the players didn't have the same passion I had, I did a lot of working out alone. I'd run the stadium steps hitting both steps simultaneously from top to bottom three times the length of the football field, running sprints for thirty minutes, and running two to three miles just to cool off. I ran until my feet, calves, hips, and lower back felt as though they were going to catch on fire. I did everything I could to relieve my charley horses and back spasms before and after I went to work or tried to sleep. I suffered most every day because I wanted to be in the starting lineup when we played Louisville Trinity High on September 5. Louisville Trinity was a perennial football power in Kentucky, and it was Kentucky's defending state champion.

My weight got up to 188 pounds; I'd never been bigger. The head coach rewarded me by listing me as a starting defensive end and the backup offensive end. I was elated.

On the first day of practice, I met the head coach, Abe Bryan, for the first time. Coach Bryan was five-one and 160 pounds. Don't let his size fool you; he was an in-your-face coach who was no-nonsense and very intimidating. He was an Ohio football legend who received visitors at our practices such as the late Ara Parseghian, the late Woody Hayes, and others.

The coaching staff prepared us for our first scrimmage with Alliance High, from a medium-sized city in northeast Ohio. Alliance produced quarterback Len Dawson, who played for the

Kansas City Chiefs and was inducted into the Pro Football Hall of Fame. I had a good showing in the scrimmage with Alliance, but the late Eddie "Rangoon" Simon had a very good scrimmage too. His impressive play and practices got him named as starting defensive end. Rangoon, a junior, acted as though he didn't want to work hard while we were training. As a result, I fell asleep at the wheel and lost my competitive edge. I was thinking that Simon had conceded the starting position to me. That was a big mistake. Rangoon's play impressed the coaches and me and earned him the right to be starting defensive end for Big Red. During the second scrimmage, Rangoon made several big plays, impressing the fans, our teammates, and most important, the coaching staff. I, on the other hand, didn't impress the coaches.

Coming into the final week of practice and facing a scrimmage that could mark the beginning of the end for me, I sprained my ankle during practice while Rangoon continued to impress everyone. I was definitely afraid of riding the bench again, but that was not an option. The summer practice ended, and we prepared for the season opener with Louisville Trinity.

Because I was convinced that Rangoon would be the starter, I told Coach Bryan my father, who was seventy-one, needed financial assistance, so I was considering a part-time job at a bakery until graduation, after which I'd apply for a full-time job at the Weirton Steel Mill. Coach told me that my plan had taken him by surprise, that I'd been looking very good in practice and had all the skills to be the starter at defensive end. He assured me the competition between Rangoon and I was very close, but he said he was going to play the best player. He said that I could be the starter again and that he would support whatever decision I made. Coach Bryan said that everyone was impressed with my play in spite of my gimpy ankle. He told me I had the heart of a lion and that I could be one of the greatest to ever play my position. With that vote of confidence, I stayed on the team. I remembered several occasions when I begged my mother to let me play football, my dream.

The equipment manager was issuing game jerseys for our season opener. I requested #84, the number my brother Lonnie wore. Moreover, #84 had also been worn by Ronnie Styles and the late, great Dwight Sims, who taught me football. Dwight Sims was one of the best football players in the school's history, definitely in the top ten. He had size, speed, athleticism, strength, and a flare for the dramatic. I wanted to play like Dwight and Lonnie. After I received #84, I felt elated, humbled, and obligated. Getting that number was the highest honor ever bestowed on me at that time. I felt obligated to play like those who had previously worn that number.

We showed off our new game jerseys at Meet the Team Night, when we met the booster club for the first time, a school tradition. After a long, hot summer of two-a-day practices, this was a fun time for the players to loosen up and clown around. After the Meet the Team Night, it was time to play.

Our opener was at home, Steubenville High's stadium, also known as "Death Valley." I arrived at school wearing a traditional crimson-colored blazer. I noticed that "#84" and motivational writings and slogans that had been affixed to my locker by the pep club. The classrooms and hallways were buzzing with excitement, and the pep club organized a rally in the gymnasium, at which some players made speeches.

After the pep rally, the players boarded a bus for the Steubenville Country Club, where we relaxed for a few hours and listened to the coaching staff go over the scouting report and the game plan. After that came a great steak dinner and a ride on the bus to the stadium decorated with signs and banners. The playing field looked like a major college or a pro stadium. We suited up. Unlike most high schools, we had four different game uniforms. Yes, we were a major program with a lot of class. We also had swag. We grazed around the field, which is, walking around to check out the field's condition and the opponent.

We came out for the final time prior to kickoff and received a roaring reception from our fans. I smelled popcorn, hot dogs, peanuts, and hamburgers. The home team's and the visitor's bands were trying to drown each other out. The pre-game music, "They Call Me Mr. Touchdown," which was coming over the loudspeakers energized me.

We did calisthenics, stretching, blocking, and catching until the referee called the team captains for the coin toss, which we lost. Louisville Trinity wanted the ball. Although I was not in the starting lineup, I had earned a spot on the kicking team. Our kicker placed the football on the kicking tee. The raucous crowd's chanting and stomping rose to a feverish pitch. The kicker launched the ball into the unseasonably warm and humid air. The Louisville Trinity deep back caught and advanced the football for a modest return. True to the scouting report, Trinity ran a no-huddle offense. Although our team was prepared and well—conditioned, this offense posed a challenge. To make things even more difficult for us, it was close to eighty degrees at kickoff, hot for early September in Ohio. Apparently, the Trinity coaching staff had scouted our team very well. Knowing that Eddie Simon was a very aggressive player, Trinity ran two consecutive plays right at him, and Eddie was sucked in and away from the point of contact on the first two plays. Trinity got two first downs.

Coach Bryan pulled Simon and replaced Rangoon with me. I was really excited and ready to go. Like a Hollywood script, Trinity ran the ball to my side, and I stopped the runner for no gain. I wanted to pinch myself to see if I were dreaming. I was making plays and impressing the coaching staff and the fans, who cheered even louder.

Trinity ran the ball almost every down without a huddle. I was having a good game until I was fooled on a quarterback bootleg; that's when a quarterback draws the defense to one side of the field, fakes a handoff, and runs in the opposite direction. The quarterback fooled me for a moment; I was drawn inside, and the quarterback ran around my end for a sizable gain. While I was pursuing the quarterback, a blocker hit me low and reinjured my already-sprained ankle. I was sprawled on the turf. After I received medical attention, my teammates assisted me off the field. The crowd gave me a standing ovation as I went to the locker room. I was through for the night and very disappointed in my injury. I'd missed an excellent opportunity to regain my starting position.

After a shocking loss, we prepared for Youngstown South. The coaching staff decided to play me at defensive end only, thinking I was more likely to suffer an injury on offense. At first, I didn't like the move because I liked the idea of catching passes for touchdowns. However, after making numerous tackles in practice while recovering from the ankle sprain, I realized it was better to give than receive—hits, that is. My ankle was getting better every day, so the trainer cleared me to play against Youngstown South. I was Simon's backup at the defensive end position. I anticipated missing a game or two, but I was happy knowing I'd be able to play and possibly get my starting position back. Simon and I played well. The Youngstown South Speedsters proved to be no match for the angry Big Red team.

In week three, we were preparing for our archrivals, the Weir High Red Riders of Weirton, West Virginia, just three miles over the bridge from Steubenville. We talked trash the entire year.

Ours was an intense rivalry; Weirton was always a very tough opponent. Although we dominated the series, any team could win on any night.

Simon started that night but made some early mistakes that led to two first downs. Coach Bryan put me in. I was fired up. As a result, I made several consecutive big plays. I recall hitting one of their ball carriers into their sideline repeatedly—I was in the zone. Surprisingly, the referees didn't flag me for my aggressive play. Rangoon didn't get back into the game until it was out of reach. We defeated Weir High 26 — 6, and my performance cemented my position as starting defensive end for the rest of the season. I used to dream about putting that uniform on, playing like the great athletes I admired, and knowing there were kids in the stands wishing they were like me.

As the coaching staff prepared the team for the Warren Harding Black Panthers, I was practicing with the first team for the first time. I was excited about my starting role. My confidence increased because I was practicing at a high level. I was determined to hold on to my starting position by any means necessary. My momentum in practice carried over into the game, which ended up being a good one for me.

I was playing remarkably well when the Massillon Tigers of Massillon, Ohio, rolled into Harding Stadium. Massillon was the only team the Mighty Big Red struggled with defeating. For some reason they simply had our number. Several losses to Massillon cost us multiple All-American Conference championships and a few state championships. We often lost to Massillon even when we had the better team.

I was really up for the Massillon game. I played almost a perfect game. I still regret my decision to fall on a fumble instead of attempting to return it thirty-six yards for a touchdown. I often wonder what could have been, but it wasn't meant to be.

I believe that the Warren Harding, Canton McKinley, and the Massillon games earned me first-team nomination to the Ail-American Conference, the toughest conference in the United States at that time.

The following week, Coach Bryan let me lead the team onto the field, being the first to burst the paper ring, the highest honor bestowed on a player. In addition to that, it was our homecoming game against Brooklyn Thomas Jefferson, a New York team. The Steubenville Big Red football program took pride in playing anybody anywhere, and our out-of-state record was phenomenal. This game was special and sentimental for me because it was my eighteenth birthday and my brothers brought Dad to the game for the first time. I was honored because Dad came to watch me play. So, I wanted to put on a show for him even though I knew he was already proud of me.

Dad sat right behind our bench, and when I came to the sidelines, I saw Dad peering around my teammates to get a glimpse of me. He was excited every time I made eye contact with him. I felt good knowing he was there to support me. I had a good but not a great day, but it's a game I'll remember for the rest of my life.

The season was winding down as the Canton McKinley Bulldogs of Canton, Ohio, came into Death Valley. The Bulldogs came in as the number one ranked team in the nation. No one but our coaches and players gave us a chance of winning. I blocked my first extra-point attempt during the game, which was a hard-hitting contest on both sides. Our hitting was so intense that we put two of their players in the hospital. We won.

We were emotionally spent when we arrived in Niles, Ohio, to play the Niles McKinley Red Dragons. They caught us on an off night. We were faster, but rainy conditions favored the Red Dragons. I almost sacked their quarterback on the play he hurled a touchdown pass. This gut-wrenching loss probably cost us a state championship. Coach Bryan was devastated. He was incredibly irritated by Marshall Gray, one of my best friends, whom the coach thought was smiling after the game. Coach vowed that Marshall would not play another game for the Big Red.

The Mighty Big Red returned home to battle its inner-city rival, Steubenville Catholic Central. It was hard to believe this was the last time I would ever put on a Mighty Big Red jersey. I was very emotional and afraid regarding my future. We were about to play our inner-city rivals, and neither team wanted to lose to the guys next door or on top of the hill because they'd remind you about it forever. As I was walking on the field, my mind went back to when, at age nine, I'd scale the fence to sneak into the game. I had realized my dream of playing for the Mighty Big Red, and I didn't want to wake up.

We trounced Steubenville Catholic 32 — 6 in both teams' final game.

Overall, Big Red had a successful season. With a couple of breaks, our team could have added another state championship to its legacy. A recap of the 1969 season is as follows:

1969 Steubenville Big Red Football Season Recap

In 1969, Abe Bryan coming off a disappointing 4 — 6 campaign the previous season was focused on getting the "Mighty Big Red" gridders back to their winning ways. However, Coach Bryan's team was surprised as Louisville Trinity, a Kentucky powerhouse and defending Kentucky State Champions, handed Big Red a 21 — 12 season-opening loss. Bryan immediately went to work by reeling off a string of victories over Youngstown South 24 — 0, Weirton 26 — 6, Warren

Harding 17—15, Dayton Roth 39— 6, Brooklyn
Thomas Jefferson 27—8, Canton McKinley 20— 14, and
Steubenville Catholic Central 32 — 6.
The Mighty Big Red played the Massillon Tigers to a
hard-fought 0 — 0 tie while suffering a heartbreaking
16 — 0 loss to another All-American Conference foe, the
Niles McKinley Red Dragons at Riverside Stadium in
Niles, Ohio.

Bryan's 1969 team featured a quick hard-hitting defense
and an efficient offense that had a balanced running and
passing attack. He beat Ail-American Conference rivals
Warren Harding, played Massillon to a tie, and beat
Canton McKinley, the No. 1 team in the nation and the
Ail-American Conference. However, Big Red's state
title hopes were literally washed away in a driving rain
at Niles McKinley. Nevertheless, Big Red established
itself as one of the state's elite high school football
programs.

The 1969 team finished 7 — 2 — 1, was ranked 8th in
the Associated Press Poll and 4th in The OVAC AAA
Division. The team was loaded with talent. Center Scott
Barren, defensive tackle Walter King, split end Bob
Washington, and fullback Tim Williams were selected
on the 1970 North-South Game and the Eastern
District All-Stars. In addition to those player selections,
defensive back Tom Mitchell and defensive end Les
Hicks earned First Team Honors on the All-American
Conference stars. Hicks, a fierce defensive end, had an
outstanding year. He was highly recruited by numerous
major college programs from all over the country.

The following article gives the reader more insight regarding Big
Red's 1969 football season.

Steubenville Red Season of Redemption

Steubenville—1969 was the year of the Miracle Mets in baseball. After here, it was the year of the Baffling Big Red in football. Steubenville finished that season at 7 — 2 — 1, but the '69 squad was one of only two grid teams in the history of the school to play Ohio powers Massillon and Canton McKinley in the same year and lose to neither one.

That team also stunned powerful Warren Harding 17—15 on a late field goal by Anthony Steiner, who was playing his first game of the year after missing the first three contests with a sprained ankle. "We never even kicked the ball much before that play," Steiner said. "It was one of those years. We came up big in big games."

Big Red battled Massillon to a scoreless tie and defeated Canton McKinley—which entered Harding Stadium ranked No.1 in the nation—20 —14 on a late touchdown. The only other Big Red team to play Massillon and Canton McKinley in the same year without losing to either one was Punque Cartledge's legendary 1931 team. That unit defeated Massillon 68 — 0 and McKinley 46 — 0, outscoring its foes 298 — 37 for the year.

The 1969 team outscored its opponents 193 — 92. The team's only losses that year were a season-opening 21 — 8 defeat to defending Kentucky state champion Louisville Trinity and a 16 — 0 loss to Niles McKinley in a driving rain. "If we had beaten Niles, we had a shot at the state title," defensive end Lester Hicks said. "We would have gone unbeaten in the All-American Conference and that would have carried a lot of weight in the polls. We were in awe over a team from another state coming into Harding Stadium in that first game.

We were supposed to play Toledo Scott, but a teacher's strike there forced us to change opponents."

Big Red finished the year ranked eighth in the Ohio Associated Press poll, yet only fourth in the OVAC Class AAA division. Receiver Bob Washington—who scored touchdowns on punt returns, interceptions, and pass receptions that year—went on to play for Notre Dame. Quarterback Gary Repella went to Ohio State on a basketball scholarship. No other players from that team went on to major college distinction.

"That team was on a level with any other teams I coached even though we lost a couple of games," coach Abe Bryan said. "Their effort was incredible. We definitely had some wins over teams that were better than us because we out-hit them.

"Our middle guard was Walter King, and he was one of our great defensive players. I remember Massillon coach Bob Cummings, who went on to coach at Iowa, telling me Walter was the first player to intimidate his offense physically. He said Walter affected their entire play-calling that night.

"We tied Massillon 6 — 6 when we were freshman and tied them again as seniors," end Rich DeLeonardis said proudly. "They never beat our senior class."

"It's funny, but my roommate at Marshall (Andre Heath) played for Massillon against us." Hicks said. "We became best of friends."

Big Red trailed Canton McKinley 14 — 0 late in the second quarter, however, Big Red got another score before halftime—when Washington intercepted a pass and returned it 75 yards for a touchdown with just four seconds showing on the clock. Steiner's 14-yard scoring run in the third quarter cut the deficit to 14 — 12. With less than three minutes remaining in the game, Big Red back Tim Williams earned a first down at the McKinley 38. Two plays later, Jeff Spahn tossed a 39-yard scoring pass to Washington, then passed to Steiner for two points and the 20 — 14 win. "Their players were lying face down on the ground when the game was over," DeLeonardis said of McKinley. "I mean, they were in shock, strewn all over the field. That had to be one of the hardest-hitting, best games in the history of Big Red football."

"Playing in the Ail-American Conference was incredible. There'd be 20,000 people at games in Massillon, Canton and Warren, and we'd pack 10,000 into Harding Stadium. All due respect to today, you don't have those intense, fierce rivalries anymore. If you won the All-American Conference, you were considered the best in the state, period."

"The hitting was so intense, we sent two of their guys to the hospital," Hicks recalled of the McKinley game. "Rocco Rich was a running back who went on to Ohio State, Lonnie Ford was an all-stater . . . both those guys made trips to the hospital that night.

"We out-hit them. That's how we won that game. Ted Boswersok was Canton McKinley's quarterback and went on to play at Kent State University.

"Our high school football was a different level then," Hicks said. "Our reserves played much more superior than any teams around us. We lived for those All-American Conference games. We were judged by them." All-American Conference all-stars from Big Red that year were Barren, Hicks, King, Williams, and Mitchell. Earning honorable mention were Ross Daniels, DeLenoardis, Ralph DeBacco, Henry Hill, Repella, Spahn and Sam Stefanidis. That was a good, all-around performance from the entire team. —John Enrietto, Sports Editor

Reprinted with permission of the Steubenville Herald Star.

1969 SEASON
Big Red Ranked 8th in the Associated Press Poll
Big Red Ranked 4th in the OVAC AA Division

1969 State Champions—AP Poll
AAA Upper Arlington
AA Norwalk St. Paul

All-Star Squad for 1970 North-South Game:
C—Scott Barren, 6-1, 198
DT—Walter King, 5-9, 195
E-Bob Washington, 6-0, 180
FB—Tim Williams, 6-0, 205

Eastern District All-Stars—AP-A A 1969 Football Banquet
Offense:
E—Bob Washington
Best Offensive Player—Bob Washington
Lineman of the Year, Best Defensive Player—Walter King
C—Scott Barren
Calvin Jones Award—Walter King

Defense:
E—Rich Deleonardis

Press Macedonia Award—Tim Williams

T—Walter King
Harry Wilson Award—Tom Mitchell
Honorable Mention—Tim Williams
Father Egan Award—Jeff Spahn

All-American Conference All-Stars

Offfense:
E—Bob Washington
C—Scott Barren

Defense:
E— Lester Hicks
T-Walter King
LB—Tim Williams
B—Tom Mitchell

Honorable Mention:
Ross Daniels, Rich Deleonardis,
Ralph Dibacco, Henry Hill,
Gary Repella, Jeff Spahn
Sam Stefanidis

All-American Conference Statistics
Top Scorers—9/11 Bob Washington, 42 points
Top Passers—6 Gary Repella, 29 of 65, 509 yards
Top Receivers—4 Rich Deleonardis, 13 — 332 yards, 2
TD;
6 Bob Washington 16-289 yards, 4 TD

All-Ohio A A - A P Poll
Offense — 1st Team —E—Bob Washington
Defense—2nd Team—T—Walter King
Honorable Mention—Scott Barren, Rich Deleonardis

OVAC All-Stars—AA
E—Bob Washington
Special Hontable Mention—Walter King, Tim Williams,
Rich Deleonardis
Honorable Mention—Tom Mitchell

Reprinted with permission of Steubenville Herald Star.

Because of the recognition I earned on the football field, I was
widely recruited by major football programs, including Nebraska,
Iowa, Ohio State, Ohio University, Kent State, Tennessee State,

Grambling, and Marshall. However, my grades weren't up to par. I had a 1.9 grade point average, so I needed to score 22 on my ACT college entrance exam but had scored only 21, just shy of what I needed to become a qualifier for a football scholarship. Some colleges told me they would hold a scholarship for me just in case I met their academic requirements.

In the event I could not bring my grades up, numerous small colleges, including Fairmont State, West Liberty, Capital, and the University of Nebraska-Omaha, made persistent calls to Coach Bryan. Believing that my opportunity to play for a major university was slipping away, I became very distraught. I hadn't worked hard enough in the classroom and was paying for it. Coach Bryan, who told me to keep my head up and stay positive, worked diligently to get me a full college scholarship.

I called a meeting with Coach Bryan to discuss my friend, Marshall, whom the coach had kicked off the team for supposedly laughing after the Niles McKinley loss. As a favor to me, I asked him to suspend his hard work regarding getting me in school and let Marshall back on the team. Coach Bryan disagreed. He said, Hicksy, I'm proud of you for sticking up for your friend. Although Marshall is an outstanding player who could help us next year, he'll never put on a Steubenville Big Red uniform again. You are an exceptional athlete with high character and you should be rewarded for your hard work. I know how much this scholarship means to you. I'll get you in school because you're going to be a great one."

My GPA remained the same. However, the University of Nebraska-Omaha made a strong push for me three weeks before training camp opened. In desperation, I made a verbal agreement to accept its scholarship. Right before I signed the letter of intent, Coach Johnny Majors of Iowa State called me. He said that Coach Bryan and Mike Palmer, one of Steubenville's all-time running backs and a former star running back at Ellsworth Community College, told him I'd be a good player for Iowa State if I attended junior college for two years.

With that, I called University of Nebraska-Omaha and told the coach I had decided to attend Ellsworth Community College. The move would give me an opportunity to develop good study habits, gain weight, and adjust to the college game. Three of my teammates, Reynard Horston, Henry Hill, and Anthony Steiner, were also headed there, and other Steubenville Big Red players were star performers at Ellsworth. I was bound for Ellsworth Community College in Iowa Falls, Iowa, though I knew nothing about Iowa.

First row: Tim Williams, Tom Mitchell, Marshall Gray, Bob Washington, Reynard Horston, Ron Henry, Ross Daniels, Scott Barret, Sam Stefanidis, Walter King, Gary Repella, Richard DeLeonardis. Second row: Jeff Spahn, Dean Young, Jim Steiner, Aaron Livingston, Mark Palmer, Lester Hicks, Ed Simon, John Nudianos, Ralph DiBucco, Joe Berardelli, Harry Cohen, Joe Stasiulewicz. Third row: Tom Williams, Glenn Hill, Ray Titus, Larry Brown, Norman Bogard, Keith Maselwitz, Mike Bauman, Lloyd Christian, Bob Radakovich, Dean Lesiak, Henry Hill, Bruce Peterson. Fourth row: Jim Wagoner, Mgr., Dave Hindman, Rob King, Leslie Washington, Mike Cara, Chris Charlas, Jack Moncilovich, Arnold Johnson, Bill McCauslen, Al DeFrances, Rich Poe, Ken Anderson, Mike Fuller, Mgr

SENIOR LETTERMEN

Bob Kozakovich, Gary Repella, Les Washington, Bob King, Curtis Fields, Clarence Bennett, Bill Elk, Tom Mitchell, Charles Wise, Howard Borden, Jeff Spahn, Steve Matusa, Les Hicks, Ted Freeman.

Undefeated

THE SEASON

Big Red	81	Weirton	56
Big Red	77	Brooke	70
Big Red	53	Canton Lincoln	47
Big Red	69	Toronto	61
Big Red	85	Brooke	55
Big Red	64	Central	59
Big Red	77	Martins Ferry	41
Big Red	66	Warren Harding	52
Big Red	100	Wintersville	42
Big Red	84	Weirton	50
Big Red	78	Bellaire	50
Big Red	62	East Liverpool	37
Big Red	67	Central	55
Big Red	66	Brooke	60
Big Red	65	Bellaire	55
Big Red	68	Salem	50
Big Red	73	Triadelphia	45
Big Red	80	Martins Firry	60

18-0

SECTIONAL CHAMPS

DISTRICT CHAMPS

National All Time Victory List (700+ Wins)

Rank	Staff Rank	School	Nickname	Wins	Win %	Overall Record
1	1	Valdosta, Georgia	Wildcats	862	.801	862-202-34
2	1	Kurt Thomas Highlands, Kentucky	Blue Birds	813	.783	813-224-26
3	2	Louisville Male, Kentucky	Bulldogs	808	.725	808-305-49
4	1	Massillon Washington, Ohio	Tigers	803	.766	803-244-35
5	1	Mt. Carmel, Pennsylvania	Red Tornado	789	.725	789-288-59
6	2	Canton McKinley, Ohio	Bulldogs	776	.700	776-326-42
7	1	Little Rock Central, Arkansas	Tigers	774	.711	774-314-48
8	3	Mayfield, Kentucky	Cardinals	773	.758	773-246-32
9	1	Hampton, Virginia	Crabbers	767	.756	767-247-45
10	1	Parkersburg, West Virginia	Big Reds	765	.727	765-287-33
11	2	Easton, Pennsylvania	Red Rovers	760	.699	760-327-54
12	1	Muskegon, Michigan	Big Reds	751	.739	751-264-43
13	1	East St Louis, Illinois	Flyers	746	.775	746-216-45
14	1	Brockton, Massachusetts	Boxers	746	.683	746-346-64
15	1	Ada, Oklahoma	Cougars	743	.767	743-300-24
16	3	Berwick, Pennsylvania	Bulldogs	738	.704	738-309-43
17	1	New Britain, Connecticut	Golden Hurricane	734	.704	734-308-51
18	1	Summerville, South Carolina	Green Wave	732	.796	732-187-25
19	2	Clinton, Oklahoma	Red Tornado	730	.742	730-253-35
20	2	Pine Bluff, Arkansas	Zebras	728	.700	728-282-32
21	3	Lawton, Oklahoma	Wolverines	727	.691	727-324-34
22	1	STEUBENVILLE	BIG RED	725	.706	725-301-35
23	4	Paducah Tilghman, Kentucky	Blue Tornado	725	.706	725-301-25

64

The season came and went. The recognition awards went to the players who had outstanding seasons. I was caught off-guard when Coach Bryan told me I had been voted on the All-American Conference First Team Defensive End. I felt I played well when I was healthy, but never in my wildest dreams had I dreamed I'd be named on the first team of such a storied conference, which was considered to be the number one conference in the nation. The All-American Conference produced famous players and coaches. Those players were Len Dawson of the Kansas City Chiefs, Paul Warfield of the Miami Dolphins, Dan Dierdorf of the St. Louis Cardinals, Willie Spencer of the New York Giants, Chris Spielman of the Detroit Lions, Marion Motley of the Cleveland Browns, Coach Paul Brown of the Cincinnati Bengals, and a host of other major college and pro football players.

The Steubenville Big Red greats were Calvin Jones, Perry Jeter, Frank Gilliam, Eddie Vincent, Don Conkel, Ron Conkel, Howard "Tiny" Linn, Harry Wilson, Leon Lindsey, Herbie Lindsey, Bob Booth, Lonnie Hicks, Raymond Terry, Don Osby, Bob Sims, Mike Palmer, Jim Smith, Keith Burke, Dwight Sims, and Ron Mazzaferra, Incidentally, Mazzaferra was my neighbor.

I was overwhelmed by my selection to the First Team of the All-American Conference, an elite group of Ohio football and Steubenville High School Big Red players. The players listed above others have left an impressive legacy as indicated by the following facts and statistics:

The Steubenville High School Mighty Big Red Legacy

Nickname: Big Red
Mascot: Man O' War (Horse)
Colors: Crimson and Black
Stadium: Harding Field, "Death Valley"

Website: rollredroll.com, will provide additional historical information.

100th victory: North End Field in Steubenville, 1925: Big Red 41, Pittsburgh St. Rosalia Panthers 0

200th victory: Death Valley, 1941: Big Red 14, Columbus Central Pirates 2

300th victory: Death Valley, 1960: Big Red 22, Columbus South Bulldogs

400th victory: Fawcett Stadium, 1976: Big Red 16, Canton McKinley Bulldogs 7

500th victory: Death Valley, 1988: Big Red 24, Steubenville Catholic Central Crusaders 0

600th victory: Death Valley, 1999: Big Red 34, East Liverpool Potters 0
700th victory: Poland, 2008: Big Red 39, Poland Bulldogs 20

800th victory?

Big Red: A state by state history breakdown.

State/District/Country	Record
Ohio	577-266-26
West Virginia	71-17-6
Pennsylvania	55-16-3
New York	18-0-0
District of Columbia	7-1-0
Maryland	5-1-0
Illinois	3-0-0
Delaware	1-0-0
Kentucky	0-1-0

Michigan   1 - 1 - 0

Ontario Canada   2 - 0 - 0

Poland (Europe)   1 - 0 - 0

Steubenville Big Red is competing in its 111th official
year of football, and 100th season (no team in 1906).
During that span, they have been 25 head coaches who
have combined to win 70 percent of the school's games.
Of Big Red's 740 all-time victories, almost half (329)
have come by shutout. Big Red is built on defense.
Head Coach Reno Saccoccia, was in his 30th season,
has coached (358), won (305), and lost (53), more games
than anyone in Big Red history. Big Red has faced 214
different opponents from 8 states, one territory and one
foreign country.

Big Red had a 43 game winning streak, and has had
winning streaks of 22 consecutive games twice. A 26
game unbeaten streak under legendary coach Charles
"Punque" Cartledge also included 17 consecutive
shutouts. Big Red's all-time playoff record is 46 wins,
and 20 losses in 23 post season appearances. Big Red's
record in overtime games (since 1984) is 7 — 2. Big
Red has had three forfeiture situations, Warren G.
Harding 1953, Columbus West 1978, and Ashtabula
Lakeside 2002. Since the State of Ohio started in 1972,
Steubenville Big Red's record is as follows:

OHSAA State Runner-Up: 1987, 1988, and 2008.
OHSAA State Semifinalist (Region Champs): 1984,
1985, 1987, 1988, 1989, 1990, 1991, 1994, 2003, 2005,
2006, 2008 &2009.
O H S A A Playoffs: 1981, 1982, 1983, 1984, 1985, 1986,
1987, 1988, 1989, 1990, 1991, 1994, 1999, 2001, 2002,
2003, 2004, 2005, 2006, 2007, 2008, 2009, 2010, and
2011.
Associated Press State Champions (Post-OHSAA
Playoffs): 1988, 1994, 2003, 2004, 2005, 2006, and 2011.

Undefeated, untied and not scored upon: 1930.

Additional Facts
Steubenville Big Red is 22nd in the Nation with All Time Victory List (700+ wins) with a 725 — 301—35 record with a .706 win percentage.

Steubenville Big Red is 3rd in Ohio All Time Victory List (Top 50) recorded with 737—302 — 35 record.

Photos and charts will give insight pertaining to Steubenville Big Red's National Ail-Time Wins and All-Time Wins in the State of Ohio.

Reprinted with permission of Steubenville High School Athletic Department and Roll Red Roll site.

CHAPTER FIVE

MOVING FORWARD

LAST SUMMER IN STEUBENVILLE

I worked in the Weirton Steel Mill for the summer after graduation to generate income for college. I worked out that summer as well because I wanted to show up in camp bigger, faster, and stronger. I worked hard because I knew the competition at the junior college level would be more difficult than at the high school level.

For fun, I'd hitch a ride with my friend, Lloyd "Brother Love" Christian, who called his '64 green Fairlane the Green Hornet or the Bat mobile. He drove our posse to East Liverpool, Ohio; Midland, Pennsylvania; and Weirton, West Virginia to get our party on. The posse included Lloyd, Teddy Freeman, Mark Palmer, Marshall Gray, then Van Gray, aka Rashid Absabur, and me. On occasion, we rode seven deep in a car without air conditioning and a rusted-out rear left floor board, but we didn't care; we'd always bring a couple of six-packs to parties. Whenever a car would pass Brother Love, he'd put the pedal to the metal but very careful. The rear passengers had to straddle the holes in the floorboard, and one slip could have resulted in a loss of some legs. Looking back, I didn't realize how dangerously we lived, but the majority of my peers didn't own a car, so I was considered to be in an elite group at Steubenville High because Lloyd had a car.

When Moe gave me a '62 yellow hardtop Thunderbird, I was a proud owner of wheels, sort of. It was more of a tease than anything else. Teddy, Marshall, and I once attempted to drive it to the North End ball field, my high school hangout. Every time Marshall attempted to drive my car (I didn't have a license), it would stall at the same spot on the north end of town. After experiencing several such embarrassing moments, I gave up on the car.

CLOSE TO THEIR LAST RIDE

One Saturday afternoon, my sister Doll and her husband, Jerry, asked me if I was ready to start driving lessons. I responded with a reluctant yes. The thought of being behind the wheel of an automobile frightened me. I don't know who was the most nervous about the idea, Doll, Jerry, or me. Jerry drove to a clearing in a remote area and gave me the wheel along with a brief orientation to how the car operated — gear selector, accelerator, brakes, and the principles of steering. It was a very hot summer day; I was sweating profusely and my nerves were on end. I put the car in gear and depressed the accelerator pedal very cautiously. I was going about ten miles per hour when Jerry instructed me to speed up. Without thinking, I put the pedal to the metal and was doing fifty in no time. I was scared. Doll and Jerry were yelling "Stop!" I did, about ten yards before going off the unpaved road. It was just not my time to die. Ten more yards and I would have driven off a sixty-foot cliff. I was in shock, and no one wanted to train me for several weeks.

After hearing about our near-death experience, my brother Willie, a brave soul, vowed to teach me how to drive before the end of the day. He gave me the keys to his black '67 Mercury Marauder and asked me to drive him downtown. That time, I was a little more at ease behind the wheel. I tried to remain calm

70

because I was driving in traffic for the first time, but I thought I was getting the hang of it. At about 1:00 PM, the parishioners of Second Baptist Church were getting out of service and the traffic started building. I saw my classmates coming out of the church, got nervous, and pressed the panic button—I accelerated and lost control. I somehow avoided hitting a parked car but ran over a curb and onto the sidewalk. Willie was yelling, and I was freaking out. The car was headed toward the house of one of my friends, Craig Murray. Fortunately, I braked before driving into his living room. I was embarrassed because of the laughter, and Willie was beside himself. He drove home, not saying a word. After that, no one wanted to get in any car I was trying to drive. I had to find another way to learn how to drive.

MY WAY

As I was coming home from work one day, I saw a 1960 white and pink Rambler for sale for $400. I told the seller I'd buy it for $350. The owner did so because the car didn't have air conditioning, and the tires were so bald you could see the air in them. We called such tires "maypops" because they could pop anytime.

I was a proud owner of my first car, which I didn't drive until traffic settled down. With no driver's license, I drove six miles into town. At first, I was a little uneasy, but I gained confidence with every mile. I thought that I'd gotten the hang of driving until I panicked. I drove over the curb, onto the sidewalk, and stopped right before driving over a steep embankment that could have cost me my life.

After that near miss, my driving skills improved substantially. I waited until it was almost midnight before heading home. On the way, a police officer was following me, and he did so for it seemed like 200 miles. My mind raced. I knew if the officer stopped me, I was going straight to jail, thus putting my football career on hold. I was nervous but cautious. When the officer sped up, I almost lost it, but he just passed me. When he was out of sight, I pulled into a parking lot and stayed there until my heart slowed down. Once that happened, I headed home again and thanked God for blessing me.

Many things could have gone wrong many times in my life, but everything always seemed to work out for my good, or at least not for my bad. I realized I could have ruined my opportunity to go to college, so I had Tom Mitchell and Marshall Gray drive me around until I got my license. I practiced my driving skills in remote areas to avoid all distractions, and I spent many hours studying for the written test; I passed the written and driving test on my first attempt.

My sister Mary gave me her car, a canary-yellow '66 Buick Wildcat convertible as a going-away gift, and it was nice, just what I needed to get to Iowa. As a result, I sold my Rambler.

Speaking of going to Iowa, I was almost a no show.

MY LIFE IN THE BALANCE

I was two weeks away from my departure to Iowa Falls. I was hanging out with Teddy in the pool hall, which, you may recall, was one of my mother's forbidden places. I was backing Teddy in a game of nine ball to generate extra funds for college. I saw that everyone in the pool hall had been drinking several bottles of pop retrieved from the pop machine right next to me; it turned out that the machine was broken and everyone was helping himself. As I walked over to a machine to see what was going on, the owner, an old woman who lived next door, walked in with a 45-caliber pistol in her hand and accused me of breaking her pop machine. She was very angry, and I was very scared. I pled my case, but she didn't believe me; she vowed to kill me. I broke out in a cold sweat when she wielded her gun. I thought my life was about to end. One of her trusted friends, however, told her I'd simply been in the wrong place at the wrong time and had not broken the pop machine. I believe this was my mother's spirit protecting me. Those words, wrong place at the wrong time, were a message from her. That was one of the most frightening experiences of my life, but I lived to pray another day.

LIVE AND LET LIVE

I had handled all my business. My bags were packed, and I was ready to start a new chapter in my life. I was very anxious and also concerned about my father. A part of Dad wanted me to go to Iowa, and another part of him wanted me to stay home. I tried to convince him I'd be okay. I told him three of my teammates were going to the same place. I promised him I would do well. I told him that after I succeeded in college I was going to take care of him because he had spent his life taking care of his children.

With all the events leading up to going away to college, I was having a hard time falling asleep. While I was trying to fall asleep, my sister Rosetta came into the house with a bloody face. She said, "I had a fight with my boyfriend." As it turned out, he'd broken her jaw and busted her lip, but she refused to press charges. I asked for his whereabouts, but she wouldn't say. Consequentially, I didn't get any sleep the night before the upcoming thirteen-hour drive to Iowa Falls.

I had to pick up my riders, Reynard Horston, Henry Hill, Jim Smith, and Mike Palmer. As I was driving down the street, I saw Rosetta with her boyfriend. I parked and confronted him, and our argument was intense. Things were getting out of hand. He was packing a gun and knife, but his weapons didn't intimidate me. My sister stepped between us to diffuse the argument; she loved this guy! I was furious.

I got into my car, promising myself that I would never get involved in a domestic dispute ever. Thinking back, I believe my sister didn't want me to do anything that would get me hurt or killed. Her boyfriend was a lot smaller than me, so he may have used his gun or knife. I left them standing on 6th Street.

CHAPTER SIX

STARTING MY FOOTBALL CAREER AT ELLSWORTH COMMUNITY COLLEGE

KEEP THE DRIVE ALIVE

I was Iowa bound. I picked up Reynard, Henry, "Baby Jim" Smith, and Mike. I drove the first leg of our journey. My drivers' license was about one month old. In fact, I believe the ink on it was still wet. I was greener than grass along the interstate, but I was up for the task. Reynard drove next, through Indiana, and we were making good time. Reynard pulled into a Skelly service station to gas up, and it was Henry's time to drive. Just after Henry go onto the interstate, drivers started blowing their horns, which woke me up. Reynard, Baby Jim, and Mike were telling Henry, "You're going the wrong way!" Henry pulled off the road immediately. He drove to a safe place on the soft shoulder where Baby Jim took over for him. That incident woke everybody up in a hurry. Baby Jim drove us halfway into Iowa. Mike drove us to Ames, home of the Iowa State Cyclones, where he was a star running back and a Second Team All-American and First Team All—Big Eight performer.

After dropping off Baby Jim and Mike at Iowa State, Reynard, Henry, and I continued on to Iowa Falls. Iowa Falls is about fifty miles south of Ames, and got there at 3:00 AM. My eyelids felt like bricks. I was exhausted, and we were lost. No one was up at that hour to give us directions, so we were going in circles.

Luckily, we saw our street. As I was looking for the address, I lost focus and crashed into a tree in front of our dorm. Fortunately, no one got hurt, but my bumper and hood were damaged. We unpacked, got into our rooms, and jumped into bed.

MEET THE COACHES

We slept until 2:30 that afternoon, took showers, and went to find a place to eat. As we were driving through town, I noticed the clean streets, rows of trees, neatly trimmed lawns, and white houses. Speaking of white, I saw a lot of white people but no black people. I looked around the restaurant we stopped at and didn't see any black workers or customers except us. This was strange. I had never been in a place where there were no black people. The town was so white even the dogs looked at you funny. At that point, I was a little uneasy. We ate our burgers and headed back to the dorm, not wanting to be late for our first meeting.

We met some of our teammates. Bob Brewster, the black running back was six-four and 230 pounds, he was going to be a load for me to tackle. He and our white starting fullback, Tom Mees, six-three and 241 pounds, had to be one of the biggest starting running tandems in the nation at all levels of football. I was wondering how I'd ever get these backs on the ground. If that wasn't enough, I spoke to a black man with a receding hairline. His full beard was showing some gray. I asked him, "Which one of these players is your son?" The man, six-four and 227 pounds, responded with a playful grin. "I'm Melvin Parker, the starting defensive right end." I didn't know if I was more embarrassed or discouraged competing with a father-like figure.

I came into camp at six-five and 202 pounds. I'd hoped to see a little playing time, but considering the size of the others, I set my sights on making special teams. Coaches and players gathered in the meeting room, and the position coaches introduced themselves. John Dornan, the head coach, introduced himself. He told us that he was from Clarinda, a small town in Iowa, and that Ellsworth Community College with his first head coaching position. He asked the black players how he should treat us. We responded, "Just like the white players." We explained the only difference between white and black players was skin color. Coach Dornan, feeling a little relieved, told us he was going to play his best players regardless of race. He gave us our practice schedule and told the team that off-campus housing would be available to all the athletes after summer camp. He told us that there were no black families in Iowa Falls; the black population consisted of 46 students, most of them athletes:

- twenty-nine football players from Ohio, Pennsylvania, New Jersey, New York, Illinois, Indiana, Tennessee, Florida, Alabama, and Iowa
- Two baseball players from Iowa
- Seven basketball players from Florida, New York, and Indiana
- Eight females from Iowa and Wisconsin

This was a culture shock for me. Just a day earlier I had left a community with a black population of 98 percent and arrived at a city where there were no black residents, except the 38 athletes and eight black females.

MY FIRST PRACTICE AS A PANTHER

Every player had to pass a conditioning skills test, including running two miles in less than fourteen minutes. I passed with minutes to spare. I ran the forty-yard dash in under 4.7 seconds. I'd been a high-jumper in high school, so the vertical jumping test was a piece of cake. I graded very high on all the tests and impressed the coaching staff because I was in outstanding shape.

My hard work over the years had paid off. When Coach Dornan told us to dress out in full pads for blocking and tackling, I immediately started thinking about how I'd get our huge running backs on the ground.

THE BIGGER THEY ARE ...

Anticipating a battle with these huge running backs, I requested every pad the equipment manager had—a neck roll, two hand pads, two forearm pads, and rib pads. They made me look bigger and let me give punishing blows. The coaching staff had me on the third-string defensive end/linebacker position. Henry Hill, a former Steubenville High teammate, was ahead of me on the depth chart at the start of the afternoon practice. Henry and I thought it was unfair to have former teammates competing for the same position because both of us wanted to start, but life isn't always fair. It would come down to a battle of the fittest.

I didn't have to wait long before tackling one of those big backs. When Bob Brewster tried to run around my end, I filled the hole and stopped him for no gain, which raised my confidence. Our running backs at Steubenville had been a lot smaller, but they ran much harder than the Iowa running backs did. I was in superior condition and more fundamentally sound than most of my new teammates. I was having a very easy time until I went head to head with Don "Big Dog" Willingham, a six-foot, 205-pound running back from Peoria, Illinois. Big Dog was built like Atlas, strong, fast, and with an attitude. He broke my tackle on two occasions. He was the real deal. He reminded me of the running backs from Massillon, Canton McKinley, and Warren Harding of the All-American Conference in Ohio. Incidentally, Big Dog was the best football player I'd ever played with or against. We ended up with mutual respect for each other's ability.

Big Dog and Felix Lobdell, Big Dog's brother-in-law, a six-foot, 199-pound running back, spent time in the NFL after college. Big Dog ended up an Oakland Raider and in the Canadian Football League via Colorado State. Felix Lobdell played for the Washington Redskins via Western Illinois. Turner Phillips, a five-eleven, 190-pound running back from Harrisburg, Pennsylvania, was another one of our talented running backs. We had the best group of running backs at any level of football competition in the nation.

Before the end of practice, I was elevated to the starting left defensive end position, which I held until I graduated from Ellsworth, while the coach moved Henry to the rover position. We won our seventh conference championship in our tenth year of junior college football with a 6—3 record. We lost to Northeast Oklahoma early in the '71 season; that team looked and played like the UCLA Bruins. Several of their players went on to play for major schools such as the University of Southern California, Texas, the University of Oklahoma, Kansas, Missouri, Nebraska, and Iowa State. Matt Blair, the outside all-American linebacker for the Hurricanes, transferred to the Iowa State Cyclones. During our game, Big Dog put Blair on his back several times. Blair wound up a multiple Pro Bowl linebacker selection while playing with the Minnesota Vikings' "Purple People Eating Defense."

The Ellsworth Community College Panthers finished the '71 season ranked as a top-twenty national team. Reynard Horston led the nation in punt return yardage three weeks into the season until he was sidelined by a season-ending knee injury. Dave Graham, a defensive back out of Peoria, Illinois, led the nation in interceptions returned for touchdowns for half of the season.

The highlight of my first season was playing at Grand Rapids, Michigan. During this time, Dad, who had relocated to Detroit, and my brothers Lonnie and Charlie braved the cold to see me play college ball for the first time. I played a decent game. It was a freezing night, and I was frustrated because the tight end and the left tackle were holding me throughout the game, but the officials never called these penalties. I lost control near the end of the game. I grabbed the player who was holding me by the shoulder pad and gave him a barrage of forearms, at least six to the side of his head, and I got called for unsportsmanlike conduct.

Coach Dornan let me have a short visit with Dad and my brothers before we boarded the bus. Dad told me he was proud of me, and his presence and love made my night. However, I didn't get any love from coach Dornan when he saw me in the game film hitting that tight end in the head. He made us run several suicide sprints until I could hardly stand up.

THE MARSHALL PLANE CRASH

At the end of my first football season as an Ellsworth Panther, the unthinkable happened. As I was sitting in my room, I saw a tragic news flash: "Marshall University Football Team Killed in a Plane Crash—No Known Survivors." The plane had been on its final approach when it hit trees on a hillside and burst into flames. According to the NTSB report, the accident was unsurvivable. The intense fire reduced the fuselage to what was described as a powder-like substance.

The memorial fountain on Marshall's campus honors this tragedy, as do a plaque and a memorial garden at Fairfield Stadium and a granite cenotaph in Spring Hill Cemetery, where many of the victims were laid to rest including six football players who could not be identified. Every year, the fountain is shutoff at the time the crash occurred and remains inactive until the following spring. In 2006, a memorial plaque was dedicated at the actual site of the crash. It read,

On Nov. 14, 1970, 75 people died in the worst sports related air tragedy in U.S. history, while a Southern Airways DC-9 crashed into a hillside nearby. The victims included 36 Marshall University football players, 10 coaches and administrators, 24 fans and crew of 5. No one survived this horrific disaster.

The movie We Are Marshall, which starred Matthew McConaughey, honored those killed and portrayed the university's enduring spirit.

THE WHITE HOUSE
WASHINGTON

September 7, 1971

Dear Coach Lengyel:

There will be a deep sense of sadness as Marshall
University football begins again this season, but it
will be mixed with warm pride that last year's
freshmen have responded so positively to the great
tragedy that struck your campus.

The 1970 Varsity players could have little greater
tribute paid to their memory than the determination
to field a team this year. Friends across the land
will be rooting for you, but whatever the season
brings, you have already won your greatest victory
by putting the 1971 Varsity squad on the field. Congratulations to you and to every member of your
team.

Sincerely,

Richard Nixon

Mr. Jack Lengyel
Head Football Coach
Department of Athletics
Marshall University
Post Office Box 1360
Huntington, West Virginia 25715

WHAT COULD HAVE BEEN

After hearing about the crash, my mind went back. Marshall
University had actively recruited me while I was at Steubenville
High. I was anticipating playing for a major college with a
winning tradition, but I considered Marshall's scholarship offer.
If I had accepted it, I would have been on the team but not on the

plane—freshmen didn't travel with the varsity then. I was deeply saddened after hearing of the deaths of the athletes who could have been my teammates.

As I was mourning the loss of the Marshall University crash victims from November through August, I had to deal with my own personal issues. Near the completion of summer camp, my roommates and I had a disagreement with our landlady. As a result, she evicted us due to irreconcilable differences. Consequently, we had to move out of our house.

HOT CROSS BURNS

At the end of camp, Coach Dornan moved me into a house with John Isom of Alton, Illinois; Delbert Connors of Alton, Illinois; Pete Ross of Waterloo, Iowa; Reynard Horston and Henry Hill of Steubenville. We formed a band of brothers relationship who had each other's back. Before we got the keys, our landlady, who lived below us, gave us some rules:

- White girls were not allowed in the house
- No loud music
- No fighting
- Keep off the grass

She told us that we'd be evicted if we violated any of these rules. Not only did most of us live more than a thousand miles away from home, but we also had to live under the scrutiny of an unforgiving landlady.

After the two-a-day practice sessions, we relaxed in our new residence, anticipating our first day of classes. Students came from all across Iowa via bicycles, cars, motorcycles, feet, and even horseback!

My courses included sociology, history, math, language arts, and remedial reading. The older players suggested I take remedial reading to get a breather from the rest of my classes by scoring low on the reading test. So, I intentionally scored low on the reading in order to show a substantial improvement when I was retested.

I aced Ms. Lorenz's remedial reading class. She was a Minnesota native in her early sixties who liked black athletes. Ms. Lorenz invited Reynard and me over every other weekend for steak and baked potatoes, our favorite meal. The rest of the black athletes accused Reynard and me of being the teacher's pets. We were. To show our gratitude, we cut Ms. Lorenz's grass, washed her car, and did any heavy lifting she needed.

Our first off-campus party was going nicely; I was drawing beer from a keg, country and hard rock were on full-blast, and the food was good. Suddenly, a large burning cross lit up the front yard. I thought I was drunk, but I wasn't. The burning cross was meant to send a message to black athletes dating white girls. I'd seen the KKK burning crosses on the evening news, but I never imagined I'd see one burning because of my actions.

Mixed dating was inevitable; there weren't that many black girls, eight to be exact on campus, and white girls were intrigued with black athletes. A few jealous white males would fire guns in the direction of blacks, write hate mail, and damage black athletes' cars to dissuade them from dating white girls. These tactics didn't work, however, because the black athletes just didn't have the option of dating within their race. Seven of the black females lived either in Des Moines or in Waterloo and would go home on weekends. The black males would have to travel to one of those cities to see a black female because Iowa had about a 3 percent African American population.

During the early '70s, many white students' first encounters with blacks were at the junior college. The only time many students had seen black people was on the evening news, and many of them perceived blacks as a menace to society. As a result, eight black athletes, including me, came up with a Black Awareness Program to educate the citizens of Iowa Falls on black culture and to dispel some myths white have about black people.

* Do blacks grow tails at night?
* Where do blacks hide their tails during the day?
* Are blacks' sex organs as large as advertised?
* Why do blacks rob and steal from the innocent?
* Why don't blacks pledge their allegiance to the flag?
* Why are blacks good dancers?
* Why do black males favor white women over black women?
* Do blacks have nine lives?
* Are blacks smart enough to play quarterback, receiver, or middle linebacker?
* Do blacks come from monkeys?
* Why are blacks good at sports?

Our open dialogue gave the local high school teaching staff and students a better understanding of black people and changed their opinions regarding blacks. For example, the parents of the girl I was dating invited me to dinner. Her parents were intrigued by the relationship I'd established with their daughter, but I was hesitant to accept the invitation. Would they lynch me? Poison me? Make me a eunuch? But after I sorted things out, I realized that if her parents meant harm to me, they could have already accomplished that by then. My friend assured me everything was cool. After getting her assurance over fifty times regarding the invitation, I accepted.

I asked Reynard to accompany me to her home, which was about twelve miles away. She lived in a nice white ranch home.

We knocked on the door, and my girlfriend greeted us while a middle-aged, good-looking couple peeked over her shoulder at Reynard and me. We exchanged pleasantries, Reynard and I freshened up, and we enjoyed a very nice dinner after her father blessed the food. My girl and her parents sensed Reynard and I were nervous, so they attempted to relax us with a little humor and light conversation throughout dinner, but I felt as though it were a job interview. However, as the night went on, the atmosphere eased. I looked at my watch and discovered that four hours had passed. I looked for an opportunity to head back. My friend's parents thanked Reynard and me for accepting their dinner invitation. Apparently, we'd made a good impression, and I was given an "open door" invitation. Her parents told me that they liked me and that I should keep up with sports. Reynard's winning personality—he never met a stranger—had them in stitches the entire night.

That was the first time I'd had dinner at a white family's house, and I'd received a warm reception. My takeaway from this dinner was that not all white people were oppressors. Bad things happen until good people get in the way, and people should not be judged by what you hear but by what you see.

I was bitter when the Klan burned crosses during our parties; it reminded me of how badly the Klan had treated my family in Georgia. As the year went on, the cross burnings finally ceased, and I saw myself maturing. I learned how to forgive and forget those who trespass against me. I had the responsibility to alter the face of racism. I couldn't change the entire world, but I could work on a little piece of it.

By the way, some white male and female students formed my fan club, "66 for Lester Hicks," a legend they put on a banner and posted at the forty-yard line during our home games. The members of the "66 for Lester Hicks" fan club gave me snacks and tutoring sessions, nothing major.

No PLACE LIKE HOME

I'd left the friendly confines of Steubenville, where almost everybody in my neighborhood looked like me, and had gone to Iowa Falls, where so few looked like me. There was no social life for blacks in Iowa Falls, which closed down before 9:00 every night. The black athletes' highlight of the evening was eating at Rocky's Pizza; otherwise, the black athletes spent most evenings in an old music room, which had a piano. The brothers would sing soul songs, play cards, and crack jokes for hours. To break the monotony, I'd accept invitations to go on hayrides and snowmobiles rides from some of the locals.

After football season, we visited Omaha, Indianapolis, Iowa City, Des Moines, Waterloo, and some other cities with significant black populations and places where they'd gather. I cannot remember if Iowa Falls had a movie theater; I never saw a movie during my two years in Iowa. The lack of things to do in Iowa made most the black athletes homesick. Some players who couldn't handle the lack of social life left school during the middle of the night because they didn't want anyone to try to talk them out of leaving the team. I believe each player thought about leaving the team every day. The lack of social activity was like prison; the black athletes would mark the days before going home to see parents and girlfriends. We read their letters every day,

It seemed like a year with no end, but the time finally came for us to go home. Most of the players vowed to finish what we'd started at Ellsworth. Reynard, Henry, and I packed up the car and drove back to Steubenville.

CHAPTER SEVEN

FAMILIAR SURROUNDINGS

We arrived in Steubenville late in the evening, and I dropped off Reynard and Henry. I could hardly wait to see my family, take a bath, and get a home-cooked meal. Nine months in Iowa seemed like ninety-nine years.

I didn't realize how much I'd missed home until I saw familiar faces, went to the movies, and hung out with my friends. By the grace of God, Weirton Steel allowed me to work rotating shifts throughout the summer.

After about a week of enjoying home, I started preparing for the next football season, working harder than ever. Here was my workout regimen:

* Running two miles
* Running the stadium steps from bottom to the top three times, 300 yards without stopping
* Run ten 10-yard sprints twenty 20-yard sprints, ten 40-yard sprints, and six 100-yard sprints
* Running a 440 backwards
* Performing the karaoke, an agility exercise where you are turned sideways and moving one leg across the other at a brisk pace for 440 yards
* Lifting weights every other day except Sundays
* Hardening both forearms by striking them against a smooth concrete wall 250 times daily
* Doing 200 crunchers daily
* Doing 200 pushups daily

My social life, work, and training seemed to eat up the summer. I wasn't looking forward to going back to Iowa. I'd thought about transferring to a college that was more socially appealing, but I decided against it because things would have gotten too complicated.

I said my goodbyes to all my loved ones and friends, packed my bags, and picked up my riders, Reynard, Henry, and Anthony Steiner, for the trip back to Iowa Falls. We got there with no incidents and greeted old and new teammates at summer camp.

MY SECOND YEAR AT ELLSWORTH

I, as usual, was in excellent shape, and I was the number one defensive end on the depth chart. Several returning players and some newcomers tried to challenge me for my starting position, but I prevailed with hard hitting and numerous quarterback sacks. I received a lot of favorable press for my consistent effort on the practice field. The news media account of the 1971 season was as follows:

DORNAN'S SECOND SEASON SUCCESS

The team improved over the 6 — 3 record of the previous year. We won eight and lost two. Ellsworth was undefeated going into the last game of the season against Indian Hills of Centerville, which we lost 35 — 0. We played Centerville in Indian Hills, Iowa, in late November in zero-degree weather. We were warmed only by fifty-five gallon drums that burned charcoal and logs. The weather was so cold that any contact on the field caused cuts and scrapes that froze. After the game, the shower room floor was covered with about an inch of bloody water, which would cause HIV precautions today.

I had to sit that game due to a torn deltoid muscle, So Rick Upchurch, an ail-American junior college running back candidate, gained large chunks of yardage in my absence.

The Panther, Ellsworth Community College Yearbook Publication

During a match up last season, Les Hicks shut down Centerville's right end sweeps. Rich Upchurch had no success gaining yardage around the end manned by Hicks. Ellsworth, one of the toughest defenses in the country held the vaunted Centerville offense to less than 200 total yards during the game.

After the game, coach Dornan was made aware of that the Centerville head coach visited the apartment of one Ellsworth player an after midnight raid in the efforts to entice the player away from Ellsworth.

The Mid Season Review

Defensively, Ellsworth is second in the conference. The defense has allowed only 10 points per game. Leading tacklers this season have been largely Smith, 62 total tackles and assists, John Garcia, 57, Scott Sickles, 52, Mike Lemon, 47, Bill Shepek, 37, Lester Hicks, 36, and Mike Stafford, 28. The defensive unit has also forced 10 interceptions. Dave Graham has caught two and scored touchdowns on both, Bill Florence also picked two. Others with interceptions are Lester Hicks, Mike Stafford, Sy Bassett, Bill Shepek, Marty Smith, and Steve Craig of Iowa Falls. All have caught one interception.

Ellsworth has put together a team this season including a trio of good kickers and punters. Don Joyce has been handling the kickoff chores this season. Joyce has kicked 29 times for 1336 yards and a 46.1-yard average per kick. Robert Cartledge has scored on 21 extra points. Steve Craig has punted 27 times for a 36.5 yard average. Team statistics tell the story about the success of the team.

EJC		Opponents
First Downs	97	57
Yards rushing	1429	739
Yards passing	879	710
Total yards	2358	1449
Per-game average	336.9	202.6
Passes intercepted	10	6
Punts	28	44
Fumbles	12	12
Yards penalized	506	699

Because of his play during the 1971 season and halfway through this season, Les Hicks going into the fourth game against Waldorf Community College was being touted as an all-American junior college candidate at the defensive end position. During the first quarter, however, he broke his left hand, but didn't want to come off the field. He managed to finish the game making several tackles, got two sacks, and knocked down a pass. He suffered through the game without disclosing his injury; he played the game in an extraordinary amount of pain. By the middle of the week, however, his pain was severe and his hand had swollen to twice its size. When the pain in his left hand became intolerable, he disclosed his injury to coach Dornan. Dornan made a doctor's appointment for Hicks, which confirmed that his hand had been broken. The doctor suggested Hicks sit out the rest the rest of the season. However, Hicks opted to play the remaining games in a soft cast.

SAD NEWS

Coach Dornan called a special team meeting to inform the team of the death of backup defensive back, John Smelcer. Smelcer's life came to a tragic end when his car collided with a bridge support right after practice. Smelcer was a great teammate whom all the players liked. We were shocked and deeply saddened after coach gave us this news. The team extended condolences to the Smelcer family.

PLAYING WITH A SOFT CAST

During our game with Estherville Community College, I rushed the passer. As the fullback attempted to block me, I leaped over him and sacked the quarterback for a big loss. I assumed the Estherville coaches couldn't believe I possessed that kind of athletic ability, so they called the same play. As I attempted to leap over the fullback again, he stepped backward, and while I was in the air, my shoe got entangled with his shoulder pad. I cartwheeled tearing the deltoid shoulder muscle when I made contact with the ground. This painful tear limited me for the rest of my football career.

My decision to rehabilitate my shoulder instead of undergoing surgery was a critical mistake. At times, the pain was so severe that I had difficulty getting dressed. During football and basketball games, my shoulder popped out every time I overextended it. This pain bothered me for over eighteen years after football.

LOOKOUT _ Waldorf quarterback Brent Thie is about to be stormed as he delivers against Ellsworth defenders. That's defensive end Lester Hicks (84) leaning, and John Garcea (76) and Rick Peterson (72).

The Ellsworth Community College Panthers were rewarded for its 8—2 season by receiving a postseason bowl bid to play in the El Toro Bowl in Yuma, Arizona. Ellsworth's El Toro Bowl opponent was Arizona Western, a top powerhouse program on the West Coast. The Iowa media reported the following events leading up to and after the game. The Iowa media coverage for the upcoming El Toro Bowl game is as follows:

Yuma Sun and Fun for Fans

After fighting 18-degree frostbite temperatures in
Iowa, the Ellsworth Panthers was ready for 84-degree
sunburn temperatures at the El Toro Bowl in Yuma,
Arizona. The sun had not risen yet as the Ellsworth
football team gathered with suitcases in hand around the
well-worn Panther bus in the wee hours of Thursday
morning, December 2. The chartered United 727 jet
winged up through the low cloud layers from the Des
Moines airport at 8:30 a.m. carrying the team, coaches,
cheerleaders and fans filling all 100 seats. The price for
the flight and 3 nights in the Flamingo motel was $200.

Signs proclaimed, "This is Panther Country" at the
Yuma airport as the Ellsworth team and fans arrived
in the warm Arizona sunshine. A free bus tour took
fans to visit San Luis in Mexico, a citrus plant that
was packing lemons under the Sunkist label and
Arizona Territorial prison. The photo showed the main
cellblock. The prison held some of the early West most
hardened criminals. The prison was maintained only a
as museums today. Marty Smith was shown enjoying
dinner at the banquet held by tournament officials and
then Yuma County Country Club for both teams. The
teams sized each other up over candlelight, fillet mignon
and entertainment by local Kofa High School choral
group. A few Ellsworth students made the 1,800-mile
trip to Yuma I by automobile. Some team members tried
the motel swimming pool after a hot practice session
Friday. Cold water kept the dip brief. Talking about
cool ones, the Coors beer truck was busy replenishing
the spigot and hospitality room for the fans.

yuma sun and fun for fans

The sun had not risen yet as the Ellsworth football team gathered with suitcases in hand around the west-wing Panther bus in the wee hours of Thursday morning, Dec. 2. The chartered United 727 jet winged its way through the low cloud layers from the Des Moines airport at 8:30 a.m. carrying the team, coaches, cheerleaders and fans filling all 108 seats. The price for the flight and 3 nights in the Flamingo motel was $500.

PHOTOS: 1. Signs proclaim "This is Pal that country" at the Yuma airport as the Ellsworth team and fans arrive at the sunny Arizona location. 2. A line bus trip took fans to the San Luis to Mexico, a shop that was selling famous goods for "booked label" and the Arizona Development prices. The prices were the early hours most railroad animals left a sunbaked sky at a sunshine tables. 3. Mary Smith is shown in the stripped field by the motel-scene pool at the Yuma country club for both teams. The teams tried each up one sandlight, live togates, and some swimmer in the heat first high school choral group. 4. A few Ellsworth students enjoy the 1894 with box on Texas by side. 5. Some sure members walking around wide swap deck after a few practice games Friday. Coach were kept decks kind. 6. Fellow share tried news. On Coach kept teams watching remembering the spirit of the Panther faithful from on the field.

statistics show that hard work pays

comments

From the fans' point of view, this football season was a test of stamina. Nearly every game was played in drizzle, wind, or fog. The serious football fan was further distracted by a noticeable increase in loud-mouthed debauchery in the Ellsworth student seating section at the home games. A possible solution might be to rate each side of the field. The west stands will be "GP" and the east stands "X" where anything goes.

season's totals

	We	The)
First downs	119	78
Yards rushing	1,768	1,126
Yards passing	1,029	798
Total yards	2,797	1,924
Per game aver.	311	214
Passes interc	11	8
Punts	38	56
Fumbles Lost	19	13
Yds. Penalized	640	650
Return yardage	902	503

Willingham, Doolin, and Lobdell lead the rushing attack.

record

Hutchinson, Kansas (here)	28-21
Fort Dodge (there)	27-14
Triton, Illinois (here)	16-16*
Marshalltown (here)	6-7
Waldorf (here)	21-9
NIACC Mason City (there)	45-7
Estherville (here)	14-0
Grand Rapids, Mich. (here)	21-14
Centerville (here)	0-35
fcl Toro Bowl at Yuma,	28-12
Arizona-Arizona Western
College

*Forfeited to Ellsworth due to ineligible player.

Team photo. L to R: ROW 1: Lester Hicks, Marty Smith, Mike Lemon, Delbert Connors, John ...

play in "el toro" bowl, yuma, arizona

team fights frostbite in iowa — sunburn in yuma

chill wind blows

PHOTOS THIS PAGE: LEFT: Charlie Davis, publisher of the Iowa Falls newspapers, takes photos while Toni Totton sits on bench with blanket due to a painful injury during most of the game. TOP: Mike Stafford (4) maneuvers as the team punted on the field. From "Spokane's Corn Bowl" as the panthers go down in defeat 28-27. CENTER: The reunion pose with team wives (?) is of Coach Worsley, John Denver, Jo and Karla Warren Anderson kneeling will trophy. Sam Osborne. BOTTOM: Dennis, Dickey and Warren Anderson find somewhat protection from the thunderous glare at the Des Moines airport while they wait for their luggage at the carousel.

Ellsworth Coach Impressed with Los Angeles Recruits

Ellsworth football coach John Dornan said that he may
start recruiting in the Los Angeles, California area.
Dornan made this observation after seeing the number
of Southern California players on the Arizona Western
college roster. Among these was Don Hubbard, a
240-pound defensive tackle who made life miserable
for the Ellsworth backfield in the Sunkist El Toro
Bowl game. Arizona Western has strong connections
with the University of Southern California. One of the
USC assistant coaches was formally on the Arizona
Western coaching staff and was guest speaker at the
Friday night bowl game banquet in Yuma. Six former
Arizona Western players who were on the USC squad
accompanied him. An Arizona Western coach said
after the game that his school really does very little
recruiting preferring to rely on rejected USC recruits
for prospects. The system obviously works quite well.

Injuries Galore, But Coach Has Special Aid

Among the "ifs" in the Sunkist El Toro Bowl was . . .
what would have been the final score if quarterback
John Tovar had not suffered a hip pointer injury
midway through the first quarter? Tovar, a sophomore,
obviously has much more experience than his substitute
John Biersner, a freshman.

Coach John Dornan's brother is a physician who was
on the Ellsworth bench for the game and treated Tovar's
injury. He described the hip pointer as a bad bone
bruise, which collects blood and body fluids. And it
hurts! Dr. Dornan put ice on the injury. He was hopeful
that Tovar would be available for duty in the second
half. It didn't turn out that way. The signal caller from
Waterloo was still in pain and Dr. Dornan kept him on
the bench. Other injuries included a broken finger for

defensive end Lester Hicks and many bruises involving other members of the team. There was real concern for defensive tackle John Garcia the fourth quarter when he was flattened trying to tackle matador fullback Vic Boniolo. Garcia was down on the field for several minutes before being carried to the sidelines. His head soon cleared, however, did not make it back onto the field.

Reprinted with the permission of Ellsworth Community College

From the fans' point of view, this football season was a test of stamina. Nearly every game was played in drizzle, wind, or fog. The serious football fan was further distracted by the noticeable increase in the foul-mouthed debauchery in the Ellsworth student-seating section at home games. A possible solution might be to rate each side of the field. The west stands will be "GP" and the east stands "X" where anything goes.

CHAPTER EIGHT

WHEN THINGS GO WRONG

At the end of the 1972 football season, I turned my attention to basketball because Erin, the three-year old daughter of the head basketball coach wanted me on the team because I was her favorite football player.

I practiced with the basketball team but didn't dress or travel with them because I wanted to leave my weekends open for football recruiting trips. I recall participating in a Friday evening practice. I was defending the post. While doing so, Bennie Clyde, a first-team all-American forward out of St. Petersburg, Florida, took offense with the way I boxed him out. As a result, Clyde and I had a verbal spat; Coach Carey and a couple players separated us, thus preventing us from throwing blows. To appease the best player on the team, Coach Carey told me to get my shower until our tempers cooled. I took a shower. As I was leaving the basketball court, Bennie told me he was going to kick my butt after practice. I told Clyde he'd better hurry because I was going to Des Moines in a few minutes. I told him if I didn't get a chance to fight him before I left, I'd come by his house as soon as I got back on campus.

When I returned, I went to Clyde's house to fight him. However, our tempers had cooled, and after a lengthy conversation, we parted with mutual respect for each other. He told me he had a lot of respect for me and admired my football play. I complimented him on his basketball talents. We became good friends for the rest of our stay at Ellsworth.

The hot-tempered Clyde led Ellsworth to a National Junior College Championship and accepted a scholarship at Florida State. One year later, Bennie and I reunited when Florida State came to play the Thundering Herd in a basketball game. Reynard, Dave, and I played cards with Bennie and the rest of his Seminole teammates the night before the basketball game and talked about old times at Ellsworth.

After Florida State, Bennie was drafted by the Boston Celtics and saw limited duty. The Celtics traded Bennie to the New York Knicks. I called Clyde whenever I got to the St. Petersburg area. Clyde, a six-eight, 187-pound forward/guard was the first coming of Magic Johnson. Clyde was the best basketball player in the country. His basketball game was a prerequisite to "ShowTime" as we know it today.

MY ONLY JOB IN IOWA FALLS

I was hired as a stocker and bagger at a grocery store, working a few hours after class and on weekends. I occasionally heard racist remarks, but I was mature enough to ignore them. Except for one day, one of the white baseball players who was my next—door neighbor said, "Boy, I want you to come by my house and clean my toilet when you get off this job." My first instinct was to beat him down on the spot, but I held my peace. As soon as I got off work, I went over to his house and punched him out. Three or four of his roommates started punching me, and I had to fight my way out of their house. I told my roommates what had occurred, and Reynard, Henry, Pete, and I went back over to their house and gave them a beat down.

THE BIG PAYBACK

The racial tension didn't stop at the baseball players' house. Because the black athletes had no form of entertainment, we tried to create our own. We used to hang out in the lobby of the girls' dormitory. One evening, a white male picking up his date took offense to one of Big Dog's playful jokes and called him a coon, which led to a fistfight. The white male suffered a broken jaw. Later, we discovered he belonged to a motorcycle gang.

A couple of days after Big Dog's altercation, a white teammate told us to be on the lookout for a group of white males planning to avenge the beating of their fellow gang member. We thanked our teammate for the heads-up and went to the cafeteria for dinner. As we were leaving, an angry group approached us, members of the motorcycle gang and other white students. They wanted to put an end to black athletes dating white girls. Some of the motorcycle gang members had firearms, blackjacks, brass knuckles, and other weapons, and some were vets. They encircled us to prevent us from getting away.

A six-nine, 290-pound, red-haired and bearded white Viet Nam veteran wanted to fight Big Dog. "Big Dog," he said, "Nigger, you broke my brother's jaw, and you're f—g our women. We're going to beat all you coons and send you back to Africa." One voice from the crowd said, "Beg for your lives, niggers." Big Dog responded, "We're not afraid of you mother f—s. I'm not begging s —t. "You're going to have to kill me." The white veteran said, "You think you're one of those bad niggers. Let me see what you got."

He and Big Dog squared off. Big Dog landed a right hook followed by two combinations, and blood splattered from the veteran's nose and mouth. That fight was over. The motorcycle gang members threw a rope over a tree limb and made a hangman's noose, again demanding, "Niggers, beg for your lives." Jim Ross said, "If you hang anyone of us, the Black Panthers will come to this town and burn it to the ground." The gang leader responded, "We don't want them coming to our town. You boys can go."

During the early '70s, the Black Panther party created fear in some white communities. Jim Ross, a politically minded, quick-thinking, militant black athlete prevented a potentially serious outcome that day because the group had been drinking and smoking marijuana. That had made them prone to violent behavior, but no one else was injured. The motorcycle gang members and many jealous white males told Big Dog they weren't through with him. In fact, they threatened to blow him up.

The black athletes held a meeting to devise a plan in the event something like that happened again. We were constantly looking over our shoulders because we were convinced anything could happen. I thought I was vulnerable because Big Dog and I lived in the same house, and he'd borrow my car frequently. I cringed every time I started my car; the gang knew how to make bombs because they were veterans. There were days when we found dead black cats at our front door with notes reading, "You are next." We ignored those tactics, figuring that if the guys had really wanted to harm us, they would have accomplished their mission. Finally, the antics stopped.

Although we encountered racism in Iowa Falls, the majority of the students and citizens treated the black athletes with respect because they loved the athletic programs, a great source of entertainment for the community.

Teachers such as Dennis Brown, Chuck Hinson, Marty Dittmer, Alvera Lorenz, and many others were committed to their professions, and I made the dean's list every semester. The root of the problem was just a few jealous white guys who couldn't accept the idea of black guys dating white girls.

THE RAPE CARD

Life was different and unpredictable in Iowa Falls. I'll share one last scare that almost ended my major college football aspirations and almost landed me in jail. Like other innocent athletes, I had to deal with an alleged rape charge. One night, I picked up a white friend I'd been dating. Her parents were wealthy Minnesotans. As I was approaching the February 1 signing day, several major football programs recruited me, except schools in the Deep South. This wasn't the case, however, with schools in the South Eastern Conference (SEC) where black athletes were not on the recruiting agenda. The SEC's lack of interest in black athletes didn't change until coach Bear Bryant's Alabama played John McKay's University of Southern California (USC). USC's Sam "Bam" Cunningham, a six-four, 230-pound running back, shredded the Crimson Tide defense. After that game, Coach Bryant stated, "I have to get some of those boys like Cunningham" and started recruiting black athletes. After he did, the rest of the SEC coaches starting recruiting black athletes, but this ironically weakened the historical black powerhouses such as Grambling, Tennessee State, Florida A&M, and others.

At any rate, my friend and I had an argument about something that we couldn't agree on. As a result, she left my room crying uncontrollably. She said that she was going to file a rape charge against Dave and me. Dave and I were very troubled. She came from money, and when money talked, black people walked. We were scared. I didn't sleep at all that night, and at some point I'd expected to be arrested. I didn't attend classes the next day because I didn't want to get pulled out of class in handcuffs.

Fortunately, late the next evening, she apologized because she didn't want me to go to jail on her trumped-up rape charge.

A HOUSE IS NOT A HOME FOR BAD BOYS

We'd grown accustomed to living on the edge. Our landlady told us that we couldn't have girls in our apartment. Unfortunately, we lived an apartment right above her. One day, she came home early and discovered that she had some girls in our apartment, one of whom was her niece. She evicted us immediately, even though it was the middle of a freezing February with snow on the ground.

Because we had nowhere to go, we called coach Dornan, who found temporary sleeping arrangements for us. Many of the residents in Iowa Falls were not willing to rent to black athletes, or they had very strict rules, such as not bringing in white girls, paying $10 a day if our rent was late, and being in by 11:00 each night. Given such stipulations, it was very hard to find a suitable place.

Coach Dornan finally arranged for Reynard, Henry, and me to move in with Don Willingham and Felix Lobdell and his wife, Vickie, and their infant daughter Felicia. For the first time since living in Iowa, we had a little freedom.

Felix, Big Dog's brother-in-law, was the only married player on the team and a creature of habit. He'd knock on my door around 11:00 PM every night to borrow my car to go shopping. Big Dog would also ask to borrow my car to run errands and pick up dates. We all got along well because we were from similar backgrounds, and we had respect for each other. We cracked jokes and played cards well into the night on weekends. To break the monotony, we used to do little devious things. One night, we raided our neighbor's apple tree until someone yelled, "Get out of that tree," so we did and headed home quickly. We were in the house a very short time before we heard a knock on the door. "Don't open it," Reynard said. A voice boomed out, "This is the police. I know you're in there." I opened the door and saw a police officer. He said, "The next time you boys want some apples, ask me. You can have all you want. And, the next time you try to steal apples, turn your car lights off. Your car lights led me straight to you." After the officer left, we breathed a sigh of relief, shared a good laugh, and went to sleep.

We were really looking forward to graduation, just six weeks away. Believing what the monkey said when it got its tail cut off, he said, "It won't be long now." We could see light at the end of the tunnel.

CHAPTER NINE

THE RECRUITING PROCESS

I hadn't made the Junior College All-America Team because some games during the season. However, I was happy for Big Dog Willingham, running back; Marty Smith, the other defensive end; and Delbert Connors, guard for receiving all-American honors. Coach Dornan gave me my All-Iowa Conference Award.

Because I was a two-year starter on the Ellsworth team with excellent grades, several major colleges started recruiting me.

I entertained football scholarship offers from a significant number of major colleges including Marshall, I discarded the letter I'd received from Marshall because I wanted to play for a larger school with a winning tradition, and I thought the team would struggle because of the plane crash.

The University of Dayton was appealing because it was about four hours from Steubenville, and I liked its defensive scheme. I'd be playing with the team's star performer, Matt Dahlinghaus, and would be coached by defensive coordinator Wally Neel, a former great from Steubenville High, under the guidance of head coach John McVay. I chose Marshall over Dayton. However, I was deeply saddened when I heard about the passing of the late great Matt Dahlinghaus, who suffered a fatal neck injury when playing Bowling Green.

The Herald Star reported on my move and granted me reprint permission.

Hicks to Transfer

Lester Hicks, a former Big Red three sports performer, will enroll at the University of Dayton next fall after completing his junior college work at Ellsworth Junior College in Iowa.

Wally Neal, former Big Red athlete who is the assistant football coach at Dayton, feels that Hicks, a 6 — 5, 208-pounder will become a starting defensive end next fall. Hicks, according to Neal, was touted as a possible all-American candidate at Ellsworth, but a broken hand, kept him out of five games. Iowa, Iowa State, Minnesota, Maryland, among others were interested in Hicks.

Neal says Hicks hopes to get a shot at pro football after graduation. He feels Hicks is of the same caliber of the young men signed off the 1971 Dayton team.

Hicks was tagged the "Praying Mantis" by his teammates. The 20-year old Hicks, son of George Hicks of 125 Locust St., Wintersville, Ohio, was on the dean's list at Ellsworth. He earned two varsity football letters, two in basketball and one in track at Steubenville High School.

Reprinted with permission of the Steubenville Herald Star

I received this letter from the University of Dayton.

University of Dayton
Dayton, Ohio 45409
Intercollegiate Athletics

March 1, 1972

Mr. Lester Hicks
1306 River
Iowa Falls, Iowa 50126

Dear Les:

Just a note to tell you how pleased and happy we are
with your decision to attend the University of Dayton
this Fall. Les, we sincerely feel you are going to make a
great contribution to our program and that you will be a
real asset to our team.

In your contract it is stated that a scholarship is for one
year and renewable for a two-year period. I just want to
give you my personal assurance that your scholarship
will be guaranteed for two years.

Les, if any questions should arise, please feel free
to contact Coach Neel or myself and again, we are
delighted to have as part of our '72 squad.

Sincerely,
John E. McVay
Head Football Coach

Steubenville High football players were accustomed to being
recruited by major schools due to its storied tradition, and most
major college programs attended our practices; that's how I got
on Coach Lengyel's radar. It was almost a certainty I'd sign with
Dayton, but Coach Lengyel at Marshall would not take no for an

answer. He suggested that I at least visit before I made my final decision, and then he said those magic words, "plane ticket." He told me that Marshall would fly me into Huntington, West Virginia, and that I could catch a ride to Steubenville with one of the students living in the Steubenville area. I agreed to visit Marshall.

When I arrived, one of the assistant coaches greeted me at the airport, and at school, the assistant coach introduced me to Reggie Oliver, the starting quarterback; Roy Tabb, the starting safety; Charles Henry, the starting linebacker; and James Street, one of Reggie's homeboys. They showed me around the campus and took me to a couple of parties where I saw Charles "Noddie" Gibson, a friend and high school football rival from Weirton, West Virginia; Darryl Miller, another friend from Weirton; and Rosenita Brown, from Wheeling, West Virginia. The people I met had varying opinions whether I should attend Marshall or not.

As I was escorted down Gullickson Hall to meet coach Lengyel and the rest of his coaching staff, I was drawn to the team picture of the 1970 Marshall University football team, the crash victims. It mesmerized me and tugged on my heartstrings. With raw fascination, I had a connection with Scottie Reese and wanted to finish what he had started. I walked down the hall but stared back at the team photo.

I had a pleasant visit with Coach Lengyel, who explained how I could fit into the Thundering Herd's football program. The visit ended on a positive note, but I was still not convinced Marshall was the program for me, except for my desire to play for Scottie Reese. I thanked everyone for showing me around the Marshall campus.

Before I caught my ride to Steubenville, I stopped at Dolen's Restaurant for a sandwich, where I saw Mary Carson, now Mary Allen. Mary was the girlfriend of Terry Gardner, Marshall's starting running back. Gardner scored the winning touchdown that gave The Young Thundering Herd its first victory after the plane crash. She did a tremendous job of selling Marshall to me. Mary gave me a different perspective about Marshall, and her input made a lasting impression on me. Upon my arrival on Marshall's campus during summer school, she made some emergency sewing repairs on my nephew's suit prior to a Jackson 5 concert.

After the three-and-a-half-hour drive, my ride dropped me off at home. It seemed I had been gone for years. I enjoyed every minute while I was at home, wishing time would stand still, but it didn't. My one-week stay was like a blink of an eye. Then, spring leapfrogged us into winter.

The following January, Reynard, Henry Anthony, and I were riding standby, flying from Pittsburgh to Iowa City, and due to a major snowstorm, we ended up stranded in Chicago for two days, sleeping at the airport. During the flight, we ran into turbulent air. The aircraft went into a tailspin. The passenger's luggage was falling out of the overhead compartment, serving carts turned over, and all the chatter dropped to a scary silence. We were afraid the plane might crash. Somehow, the pilot regained control of the aircraft and flew out of danger. Everyone breathed a collective sigh of relief.

As the recruiting process continued, I weighed the pros and cons about Marshall, and the cons outweighed the pros. I visited the University of Maryland and Kent State. I really liked what Coach Jerry Clairborne was doing at the University of Maryland. The school had excellent weight training and nutritional programs, and I was excited about playing with Randy White, a defensive star and an eventual Dallas Cowboy; Bob Avellini, who wound up playing for the Chicago Bears; and Tim Wilson, a fullback who had a long NFL career with the Houston Oilers. I liked Kent State because it was less than two hours from home, but I still favored a larger school.

The pressure of being a top recruit started to weigh on my nerves. The coaches recruiting me were all very nice, and I didn't want to say no to anyone. As a result, this made my decision more difficult. Therefore, I took their calls and decided to cancel the rest of my campus visits because I was getting behind at school and wanted to minimize pressure.

The recruiting trips had gotten me out of Iowa Falls and onto other campuses leading up to signing day. I had many sleepless nights. I was torn between my desire to attend a school with a major college football program to go to Marshall University and play in Scottie Reese's honor, and to attend Dayton, a school that really wanted me as well. Although I was in a win-win situation, I didn't want to tell any coach no.

On signing day, I had narrowed my choices to Marshall and Dayton and was leaning toward Dayton. The telephone rang. Coach Lengyel reemphasized, "A lot of schools want you, but we need you. I want you to help me rebuild the Marshall Football program. Although there'll be challenges, you'll have the opportunity to do something special." Coach Lengyel sold me on Marshall.

Just minutes later, coach McVay called with the news that he was about to board a plane to come out to sign me. I told him I had committed to Marshall and apologized to him. Although I should have been happy about signing with Marshall, I felt I had let Coach McVay and coach Neel down. What's more, I liked the idea of playing in my home state, familiar surroundings, with a coach from my old high school.

MY UNIVERSITY LETTERS

University of Notre Dame
Notre Dame, Indiana 46556
Ara Parseghian
Head Football Coach

October 5, 1971

Mr. Lester Hicks
1306 River Street
Iowa Falls, Iowa

Dear Lester:

Your name has been recommended to the University of
Notre Dame as that of a possible student-athlete. To aid
me in my recruiting procedures, I would appreciate you
filling out the white questionnaire and having your coach
fill out the blue questionnaire before returning them to
me. Upon receipt of these forms, I will have begun a file
of information on you and will be able to follow your
progress throughout your remaining junior college career.

Faith, desire, sacrifice and a positive attitude are a few
ingredients necessary for you to achieve your goals in
life. Education is the key. Possess and maintain these
aforementioned ingredients while in the classroom, as
well as on the field.

Upon conclusion of your senior football season, I
will contact you and request game film for evaluation
purposes.

Best wishes for success in all endeavors.

Sincerely,
Tom Pagna
Assistant Football Coach

Syracuse University
Department of Athletics
Manley Field House
Syracuse, New York 13210

January 13, 1972

Mr. Lester B. Hicks
Ellsworth Junior College
1306 River
Iowa Falls, Iowa 50176

Dear Les:

We have taken the liberty of forwarding to you an application that we would like you to complete and return to our Admissions Office at your earliest convenience.

At the present time we have a former member of the Steubenville High School football team, Tim Williams, who is a student-athlete here at Syracuse. If you feel that in the future you would like to further your education at an eastern school which would be close to your hometown of Steubenville, Ohio, we would like you to return the application.

It will be necessary for you to be accepted academically at Syracuse before you can be considered for any aid in terms of an athletic scholarship.

If this meets with your approval, please indicate your interest in Syracuse to us.

I will look forward to hearing from you in the near future.

Kindest regards.

Sincerely yours,
Joseph J. Krivak
Assistant Football Coach

Department of Athletics
Colorado State University
Fort Collins, Colorado 80521

Dear Student-Athlete:

Your name has been recommended to Colorado State
University as that of a possible student-athlete. Please
excuse this form letter as we are merely trying to
establish a record on any prospect who is genuinely
interested in pursuing an education and continuing his
athletic career.

Colorado State University is located in Fort Collins,
Colorado, which has a population of approximately
46,000. The student enrollment at CSU is currently
17,000. We have eight undergraduate colleges to serve
you. It is possible to prepare a young man for almost
any profession he might desire to enter. We have a
tremendous student body and faculty, which is of
utmost importance to you. We are a member of the
Western Athletic Conference, an exceptionally well-
respected major university conference. Our new four
million dollar athletic complex leaves little to be desired
as far as facilities to make your football career most
enjoyable and productive. We have five new football
practice fields, three of which are lighted. The latest and
most important phase of our new construction is the
completion of our new 30,000 seat Hughes Stadium,
which is located in the foothills section of our campus.
A model of this stadium was chosen to be on exhibit at
the 1968 Olympics as the most ideal college stadium in
modern times.

We are eager to learn more about you. Primarily, this
all begins with our questionnaire that we have enclosed.
After we receive your questionnaire, we will follow
your progress this fall. Our format for selection of
scholarship winners is based on several items; grades,
transcript, playing film and personal interview. I
sincerely hope you will consider Colorado State

University as the institution of higher learning for your future educational and athletic plans. I will be looking forward to hearing from you in the very near future.

Sincerely,
Assistant Football Coach

Boise State College
Athletic Department
1907 Campus Dr.
Boise, Idaho 83707

December 28, 1971

Lester Hicks
Ellsworth College
Iowa Falls, Iowa 50126

Dear Lester:

We have heard a lot of good things about your football ability in junior college and would like to congratulate you on your past performance.

We are vey interested in you as a potential player for Boise State College and would like to get some basic information for our files. Please fill out the enclosed questionnaire and return it to us at your earliest convenience.

We will be in touch with you personally in the near future; and, in the meantime, if you have any questions regarding our program or area, please do not hesitate to contact me.

Sincerely yours,
Adam Rita
Assistant Football Coach
Boise State Broncos

The University of South Dakota
Vermillion, South Dakota 57069

October 29, 1971

Mr. Lester Hicks
Ellsworth Jr. College
Iowa Falls, Iowa

Dear Lester:

You have been recommended to us as one of the
outstanding college football prospects in your area.
We hope you are planning to continue your education,
and if so, that you will consider the educational
opportunities at the University of South Dakota.

The University of South Dakota is one of the finest
universities in the nation. Our schools within the
University offer degrees in practically any field
that you would be interested in. Our enrollment is
approximately 5,000 students.

So that we can become better acquainted with you,
kindly complete and return the enclosed questionnaire
as soon as possible. Please note that the ACT score will
be needed prior to acceptance to an N.C.A.A. school.

If you have any questions regarding our University or
our athletic program, please send your inquiry to me.

Good luck in the remainder of your senior year. We
hope to hear from you soon.

Sincerely,
Al Johnson, Assistant Football Coach

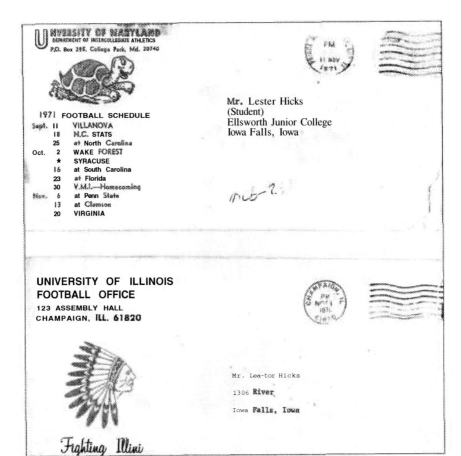

UNIVERSITY OF MARYLAND
DEPARTMENT OF INTERCOLLEGIATE ATHLETICS
P.O. Box 295, College Park, Md. 20740

1971 FOOTBALL SCHEDULE

Sept.	11	VILLANOVA
	18	N.C. STATS
	25	at North Carolina
Oct.	2	WAKE FOREST
	★	SYRACUSE
	16	at South Carolina
	23	at Florida
	30	V.M.I.—Homecoming
Nov.	6	at Penn State
	13	at Clemson
	20	VIRGINIA

Mr. Lester Hicks
(Student)
Ellsworth Junior College
Iowa Falls, Iowa

UNIVERSITY OF ILLINOIS
FOOTBALL OFFICE
123 ASSEMBLY HALL
CHAMPAIGN, ILL. 61820

Fighting Illini

Mr. Lea-tor Hicks

1306 River,

Iowa Falls, Iowa

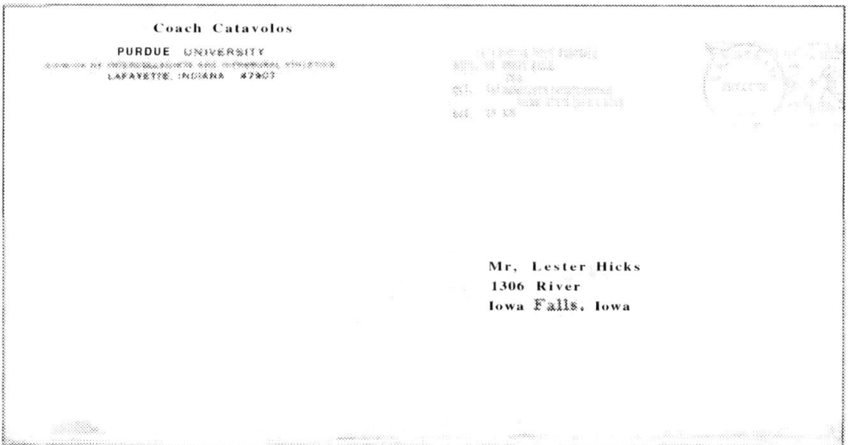

Coach Catavolos

PURDUE UNIVERSITY

LAFAYETTE, INDIANA 47907

Mr. Lester Hicks
1306 River
Iowa Falls, Iowa

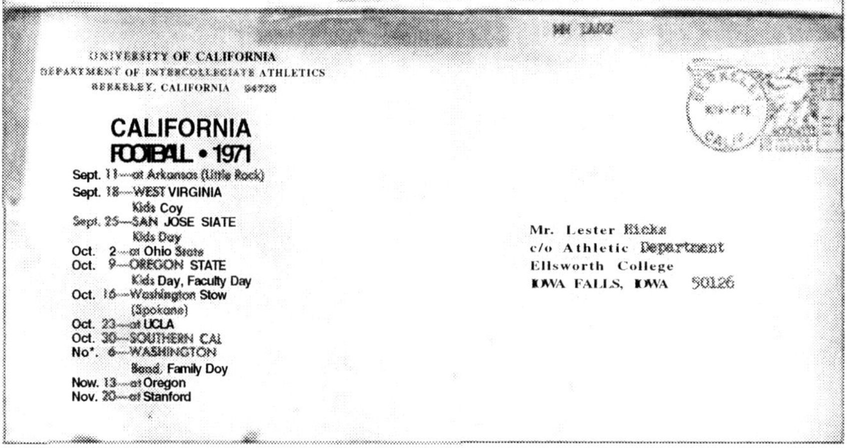

UNIVERSITY OF CALIFORNIA
DEPARTMENT OF INTERCOLLEGIATE ATHLETICS
BERKELEY, CALIFORNIA 94720

**CALIFORNIA
FOOTBALL • 1971**

Sept. 11—at Arkansas (Little Rock)
Sept. 18—WEST VIRGINIA
　　　Kids Coy
Sept. 25—SAN JOSE STATE
　　　Kids Day
Oct.　2—at Ohio State
Oct.　9—OREGON STATE
　　　Kids Day, Faculty Day
Oct. 16—Washington Stow
　　　(Spokane)
Oct. 23—at UCLA
Oct. 30—SOUTHERN CAL
No*.　6—WASHINGTON
　　　Band, Family Day
Now. 13—at Oregon
Nov. 20—at Stanford

Mr. Lester Hicks
c/o Athletic Department
Ellsworth College
IOWA FALLS, IOWA　50126

VERSITY OF UTAH
IC DEPARTMENT SALT LAKE CITY, UTAH 84112

Lester Hicks
c/o Coach John Dorson
Ellsworth Junior College
Iowa Falls, Iowa 50126

INTERCOLLEGIATE ATHLETICS
NIVERSITY of DAYTON
DAYTON, OHIO 45469

Lester Hicks
1306 River
Iowa Falls, Iowa 50126

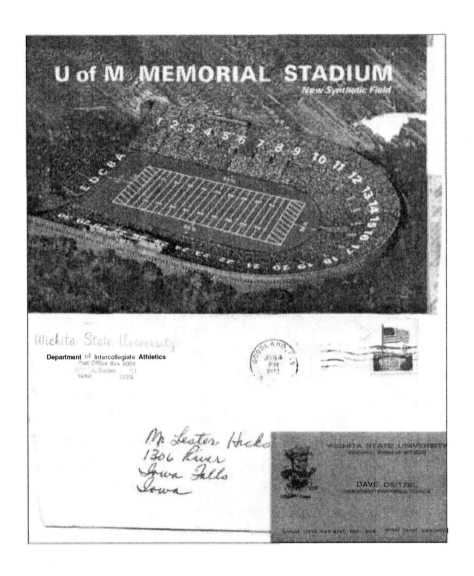

Marshall University
Department of Athletics
Huntington, West Virginia 25715

April 11, 1972

Mr. Lester Hicks
Ellsworth Junior College
Iowa Falls, Iowa

Dear Lester:

Congratulations on your decision to attend Marshall
University. The next four years will be extremely
important ones for you. You will have the opportunity
to achieve a fine education and although, at times, the
academic load will be very demanding, the results will
be most gratifying.

We believe that Marshall University will afford you
an opportunity to realize your greatest potential
academically, athletically, and socially.

We will be sending you our Summer Conditioning
Program in July. Because of the limited time and the
amount of work to be accomplished, it is of utmost
importance that you report to practice in top physical
condition.

Freshman football players are many times an unknown
quantity. High school reputations and publicity releases
cannot predict how a high school senior football player
will react to the intensified competition at the college
level. Some boys with strong high school reputations
will not meet the challenge and others less publicized
will enjoy exceptional success. If you have football
courage and a dedication to the sport that can continue
in college, with no adverse effect on your academic
program, you will be a standout player at Marshall

University. Your football attitude and the football attitude of your teammates when we start practice next fall will determine the success of our team.

Congratulations again and our entire staff welcomes you as a member of the "Young Thundering Herd" football.

Sincerely,
Jack Lengyel
Head Football Coach

Who's Who Among Students in American Junior Colleges
March 10, 1972

Mr. Lester Hicks
1306 River
Iowa Falls, Iowa 50126

Dear Mr. Hicks:

I am happy to inform you that you have been nominated for you campus for inclusion in the 1971-72 edition of Who's Who Among Students in American Junior Colleges and that your nomination has been accepted by the editors.

This honor is conferred annually upon outstanding student leaders from approximately 800 junior colleges in the United States. In selecting candidates, campus nominating committees are instructed to choose those students whose academic standing, service to the community, leadership in extracurricular activities, and future potential are decidedly above average.

As documentary evidence of this honor and in recognition of your accomplishments, a certificate will be presented to you on campus later this year.

In addition, you are invited to make use of a special reference/placement service maintained to assist nominees seeking post-graduate employment, admission to four year colleges and universities, the Peace Corps, International Voluntary Service, or any other similar position. There is no charge for this service, for the certificate, or for inclusion in the publication.

The questionnaires included with this letter are for the preparation of your entry in the publication and to provide background material for the placement service. The enclosed instruction sheet explains the nature of each more fully.

Please complete and return these questionnaires immediately.

On behalf of our staff and myself, I would like to compliment you on your outstanding work and to congratulate you on your accomplishments for which you will be included in this year's edition of Who's Who Among Students in American Junior Colleges.

Hoping to hear from you in the near future, I remain.

Sincerely,
H. Pettis Randall
Director

CHAPTER TEN

How I OVERCAME ADVERSITY

RECOGNITION IN THE CLASSROOM

Although I had a lot of success on the gridiron, I was more proud of my academic achievements. I had made the dean's list both years at Ellsworth and ended up in Who's Who Among Students In American Junior Colleges. I cherish this award because it validated me as a student-athlete and created opportunities for me to be recruited by major colleges for academic and athletic abilities. I was determined not to repeat the mistakes I'd made in high school.

GRADUATION DAY AT ELLSWORTH

My two years at Ellsworth made me grow up very fast. I had to endure many lonely nights, I saw racist crosses burned on a frequent basis, I survived a potentially dangerous mob, I suffered an assortment of injuries, and I sweated out a made-up rape charge. Nonetheless, I fulfilled a promise I'd made to my mother by earning a college degree and accepted a full football scholarship at Marshall. I thanked God for bringing me out of unbelievable trials and tests in Iowa, and I knew many people were praying for me. For that reason, I gave God the glory for placing a hedge around me.

On June 3, 1972, I was happy as a lark. I'd just received an associate of arts degree from Ellsworth. I thanked God for all the people who had helped me attain my goal and had seen me through so many troubles. I was deeply saddened because my mother was not there to see me graduate. To be honest, there were many times I'd thought about quitting, but that was a habit I refused to let myself get into.

After I picked up my degree, I said good-bye to my teammates and classmates, most of whom I knew I would never see again. I was going to miss them, but I wasn't going to miss the drama. The car was filled with Reynard, Reynard's dog, LA, Henry, and Anthony. We drove off between endless rows of corn and soybean fields and closed the chapter on Iowa. To date, I have yet to return. However, getting back home was not as easy as you would have thought.

GOING BACK HOME — NOT EASY

While we were driving through Illinois, I noticed that the rear end of the car was smoking. I panicked; would the car catch on fire? I drove to a repair shop in Leroy. The mechanic told me that my brake shoes and drums were cherry red with heat and needed to be replaced. The mechanic told me that we had overloaded the car, thus causing the brake system to wear excessively. He charged almost $300, a lot for college students, but we had to pay. We pooled our resources and were once again on our way.

The long delay had tired us out; we were fatigued. We had a mental lapse as we tried to leave Indiana and enter Ohio, and we missed our exit repeatedly. I can't count how many times we kept going in circles, but I can tell you our thirteen-hour drive turned into a twenty-three hour drive Nevertheless, we made it home.

CHAPTER ELEVEN

A DATE WITH DESTINY

Looking back, I believe I was destined to attend Marshall University. I had wanted to play in a major football conference, and Marshall was not a high-visibility football program during the late '60s, '70s, or early '80s. When I was growing up, I watched college football on TV and fantasized about catching the winning touchdown or making a game-saving tackle for Notre Dame, Nebraska, or some other major college team. Several former Steubenville Big Red athletes were playing football for many great schools.

I first heard about Marshall when they sent me a prospect letter during my senior year at Steubenville, but my teammates said Marshall had a losing tradition, and Steubenville athletes were used to winning. However, the plane crash and my campus visit had changed my mind. I felt obligated to finish what Scottie Reese had started at Marshall, and I was at peace with my decision to play for the Young Thundering Herd. When I signed on with Marshall, I didn't realize I had become a part of history and would be writing about it forty-two years later.

Outlook for 72
Coach Lengyel's Comments

General: Success for Marshall's 1972 squad will hinge upon the improvement of 31 returning lettermen and the abilities of incoming freshmen and junior college prospects. Under head coach Jack Lengyel, the Thundering Herd notched a 2—8 record in 1971. With 28 of those 31 returning letter winners, freshmen and sophomores last fall, those two wins were quite an achievement.

The 1972 campaign will be another difficult one with several problem areas still remaining. The newcomers, both freshmen and the JC standouts, must be able to bolster the Herd's interior lines.

"We are optimistic about this season, even though we are still basically an underclassmen varsity football team. We are a year older and improved, but thin at several positions. The schedule is the same as last year except we won't surprise anyone. No one should take us too lightly."

Strengths: The 31 lettermen returning will be the Herd's main strength, even though most are sophomores and juniors. "Our strengths lie in the defensive secondary, offensive backs and receivers. We have reasonable experiences, depth and quality in these areas."

Weaknesses: A recruiting concentration on interior linemen reveals a weakness of the squad. "Both offensively and defensively, our interior lines are thin in number and size. Linebackers also are a source of concern."

Offense: The Herd will switch from the Veer offense of last season to an I-formation attack. "We'll run out of the I—formation and concentrate on a ball-control type attack. Last season, our defense was on the field too much, we've got to sustain our drives.

Defense: Marshall will operate with a variety of defensive formations, utilizing the Oklahoma, 4 — 3, etc. The interior defensive linemen will be termed guards and tackles, with one end and two linebackers, two cornerbacks, a rover back and a free safety.

Major Losses: Only four seniors and two starters will be missing. Nate Ruffin and Gary Morgan, both starters at defensive backs, reserve linebacker Dave Smith and reserve center Mike Swartley are gone.

Top Returnees: Thirty-one letter winners are back, led by most valuable back Charles Henry, linebacker, and most valuable lineman, Chuck Wright, defensive guard. Tight end Randy Kerr and wide receivers Lanny Steed and Dick Washington along with running backs Terry Gardner, Ned Burks and John Johnstonbaugh are all returning. Henry and Wright head the list of defenders back, along with safety Gene Nance, middle guard Odell Graves and linebacker Rick Meckstroth.

Top Newcomers: Several freshmen could move into the picture in the offensive interior and defensive front. Two Ellsworth Junior College newcomers, 6-2, 220 Delbert Connors and 6-6, 215 Lester Hicks could be possible starters in the lines. Transfers Joe Wizba, defensive end, and Sam Twardoski, quarterback, could figure in the picture.

Spring Surprises: Eric Gessler moved into the starting center position and performed well. Transfer Joe Wizba operated as a starter at defensive end. Quarterback Sam Twardoski was progressing well until a knee injury sidelined him.

Position Changes: Dick Washington, a split end last year, has been moved to flanker or slot-back. He'll be carrying the ball some this year. Bill Wright was moved from center to guard and Ed Carter from offensive to defensive guard. Charles Henry, a linebacker, will operate at rover, as will Tom Bossie, former tight end.

Offensive Line: Youth combines with experience on the offensive line. Eric Gessler returns at center and captain Jack Crabtree and Bill Wright are set at the guards. Sophomore Larry Call and Mark Brookover hold the edge at tackle.

Receivers: The leading receiver of the past two seasons, Lanny Steed, promises to be a fixture at split end with Randy Kerr returning to the tight end. Bill James, of Herd basketball fame, could see a good deal of action as a receiver.

Quarterback: Two-year starter Reggie Oliver is the first string quarterback. Bob Eshbaugh, moving from fullback, could challenge David Walsh for the number two slot.

Running Backs: Sophomore Jim Wulf is back at fullback with John Johnstonbaugh challenging for a berth. Terry Gardner and Jon Lockett will fight it out at tailback, and flanker is up for grabs between Ned Burks, Bob Krone, and Jim Mercer.

Defensive Line: John Shimp and Bob Westfall are listed as the top candidates at end, followed by Lester Hicks and Fred Bader. Chuck Wright, Most Valuable Lineman the past two seasons, is back as tackle along with Allen Meadows. Ace Loding is expected to be the middle guard.

Linebackers: Rick Meckstroth and Mark Miller, a pair of seniors, return as The Herd linebacker probables.

Secondary: Charles Henry moves from linebacker to cornerback to anchor the secondary. Sidney Bell is at the other corner, and Tom Bossie takes over at roverback with Roy Tabb the safety.

Specialty: Larry McCoy, last season's top scorer, is expected to handle the field goals and extra points. Eshbaugh is the most likely punter.

Herd Awards

1972: Most Valuable Back—Lanny Steed (Offense), Charles Henry (Defense)
1972: Most Valuable Lineman—Jack Crabtree (Offense), Chuck Wright (Defense)
Spring 1973: Most Improved Back—Sidney Bell
Most Improved Lineman—Larry Call
"Hustler" Award—Jim Wulf
Spring Game MVP—Reggie Oliver

This was the first media coverage involving me at Marshall. I came into the 1972 camp listed as the backup defensive end on the depth chart.

Reprinted permission was granted by Marshall University's Athletic Department to reprint this information.

GETTING READY FOR TRAINING CAMP

After signing with Marshall, I spent my summer in Huntington, West Virginia, working for Diniaco & Sons Painting Contractors. When I rolled into Huntington, it was a late June afternoon, a little after 3:00 PM. The heat was breathtaking. I stopped at a service station to get directions to East Towers on the Marshall's campus. The attendant's took me to the East Towers Dormitory.

The East Tower was positioned in an ideal location, the middle of Marshall's campus. The workout facility was across the street, downtown was a ten-minute walk, and my work was about a ten-minute drive. I unpacked and called Reggie Oliver, who came by to give me a tour of campus and Fairfield Stadium.

Fairfield Stadium was where Marshall home games were played until "The Joan" replaced it during 1999. Reggie and I discussed Coach Lengyel's summer conditioning drills, which were hard. We wanted to follow them religiously.

Reggie and I started working out when I got off work. Reggie had an extraordinary work ethic and was a confident, natural-born leader. No matter how tired we were, we didn't cut corners because we wanted to be in excellent shape when training camp started. We executed our workouts outside Gullickson Hall daily. In addition to our workout, I ran fifteen flights of steps in my dorm at least three times every night. On occasion, I saw Mary Carson sitting in the dorm's lobby where she would give me a word of encouragement prior to my workout.

Reggie and I often said no to the cafeteria food and treated ourselves to Frank's steak sandwiches and fries or the hot dog special, sometimes both. Frank's had the best Philly steak sandwiches on the planet. Reggie introduced me to several friends of his friends, including Kenny Slaughter, Rick Hoverous, Buddy Jackson, Charles Dozier, Jonathan Williams, Tim Meadows, Tommy Murrell, Pee Wee Murrell, Ed Murrell, Timothy Diggs, Dallas Jones, the late George Stone, the late Dave Smith, Sheila Callahan, Teresa Harmon, Beverly "BJ" (now Murrell), and Billy Boyd. All were on campus or living across town, but Reggie and I didn't care much about socializing—we were focused on getting in shape to win games.

After completing Coach Lengyel's required conditioning drills, I used to run routes for Reggie to give him an opportunity to strengthen his arm. Running pass routes increased my speed and stamina. Before we knew it, the entire team arrived for two-a-days and sometimes three-a-days. I appreciated every football practice because like life, the day would come when I wouldn't be able to practice anymore, just like the day when I would take my last breath.

Coach Lengyel required every player to run two miles inside twelve minutes. Reggie and I didn't have any problem with that, but some players struggled. Everyone was waiting for the forty-yard dash trials; it was rumored we had one player who could do it in 4.3 seconds. When the coach said, "Ready, set, go," the subject player ran a pedestrian 4.8.

However, a couple of days later, the late Jon "The Rocket" Lockett reported to camp, and his 40-yard dash time was close to that exclusive 4.3 club. He was sporting a big Michael Jackson afro wig. Although nobody said anything, we were wondering what was up with that. Coach Lengyel, sensing this, called a meeting at which he explained that Jon had a rare disease that removed all his body hair and left him feeling sensitive about it. He'd even thought of quitting the team out of embarrassment. Coach told us to avoid staring at Jon and refrain from making insensitive comments. Coach Lengyel asked Reggie Oliver, Roy Tabb, Charles Henry, and me to look after Rocket to ensure he felt comfortable and a valued member of the team. The players loved Rocket, one of the team's top running backs. He was all right until he attempted to catch one of Reggie's passes, which had a little mustard on it. It broke Rocket's finger; Reggie had a cannon for an arm. Reggie and another of my quarterback friends, the late Joe "Jefferson Street" Gilliam of the Tennessee State Tigers and Pittsburgh Steelers, had two of the strongest arms in the nation.

Rocket shook his injury off, and the Young Thundering II prepared for our archrival, Morehead State in Kentucky during the dog days of summer. Fairfield Stadium's artificial playing surface was about ten feet below the stands and could get up to 114 degrees on the practice field. The facilities department built an air conditioning booth for the players when they came off the field. The training staff gave us water and sprayed us down with water when our pads were removed. These precautions kept us hydrated. In spite of the training staff's effort, several players, including me, had to be treated for dehydration. Those who got dehydrated or lost too much weight, 5-6 pounds were held out of the next practice. We practiced from 8:30 to 11:30, 3:30 to 5:30, and 8:00 to 9:00. We enjoyed the air conditioning booth throughout summer camp and the first two games, until our opponents filed a complaint with the NCAA, and we had to remove it.

Everything was going well until I went to student orientation and missed morning practice. During afternoon practice, I was out of position and blew my coverage assignment. My mistake infuriated the defensive coordinator. "You missed practice for an orientation! I don't need you, hotshot. If you don't like it, transfer to one of those big schools like Notre Dame, Maryland, or Syracuse." I was embarrassed and crushed. I walked off the field, wondering where I could transfer.

Coach Nameth, however, asked the defensive coordinator if he could work me in with the defensive line. He started me working with the defensive tackles, but I was undersized, and the constant fighting through double teams aggravated my partially torn deltoid. However, I was willing to try defensive tackle because I just wanted to play. Besides, if Charles Henry, who weighed about 170, played middle linebacker, I could give defensive tackle a shot. I worked out with the defensive tackles for a while and ended up as a starting defensive end.

The defensive tackle position took its toll on my ailing shoulder. The trainer, Vic Winburn, used three rolls of tape and an adhesive spray to secure my left shoulder before every practice. The tape hurt when I took it off, and it tore off my chest hairs and skin. I'd bleed in the shower, and the soap and water stung my scrapes. A few weeks later, when my shoulder harness came in, it was like Christmas. This harness was my best friend, and I wanted to take it back to my dorm.

During the two-a-days, my pain was bad. I used to dread the alarm going off, and I had difficulty washing my back in the shower because my left arm was tight and sore, and I had trouble getting dressed, as my left arm often felt numb. I wore slip-ons to avoid having to tie my shoes. I'd hobble to the cafeteria, where I had to balance my tray on my right hand.

You know, however, whenever I got to the locker room, got undressed, and got my ankles and shoulder taped, the pain seemed to go away. In spite of my debilitating injuries and illnesses, I didn't miss more than five practices in my whole football life, fourteen years. I had a passion for the game. When I stepped on the practice field, my mind was in a place where nothing else mattered. The pain didn't matter until I walked off the field. I received treatment and pressed on.

I had a high threshold for pain and an incentive to keep playing because I had dedicated my play for Scottie Reese. Putting someone ahead of myself set me up for success. It was as if a supernatural power had given me the will to do things others would have deemed unimaginable. God rewarded me because I was thinking of someone else. When you do well for someone else, you will receive countless blessings.

THE START OF THE 1971 FOOTBALL
SEASON AT MARSHALL

THE YOUNG THUNDERING HERD II - 1972

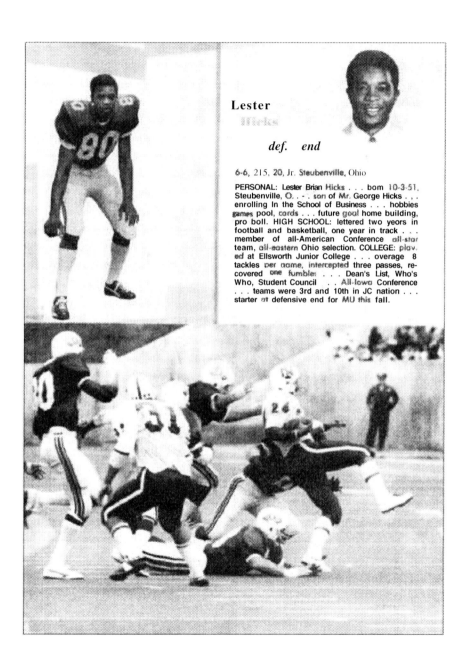

Lester Hicks

def. end

6-6, 215, 20, Jr. Steubenville, Ohio

PERSONAL: Lester Brian Hicks . . . bom 10-3-51, Steubenville, O. . - . son of Mr. George Hicks . . . enrolling In the School of Business . . . hobbies games pool, cards . . . future goal home building, pro boll. HIGH SCHOOL: lettered two yeors in football and basketball, one year in track . . . member of all-American Conference all-star team, all-eastern Ohio selection. COLLEGE: play. ed at Ellsworth Junior College . . . overage 8 tackles per game, intercepted three passes, recovered one fumble . . . Dean's List, Who's Who, Student Council . . All-Iowa Conference . . . teams were 3rd and 10th in JC nation . . . starter at defensive end for MU this fall.

Northern Illinois vs. Marshall in 1972 Season

I was given permission from the Marshall University Athletic program to reprint their photos.

In the locker room, the coaches went over Morehead State's game plan while I was wondering some crazy things. What if I tripped while running down the steep incline into the stadium? What if the PA announcer forgets to call my name? I was told that some Marshall fans could be harsh. Some fans called us the "Blundering Turd" and said we played in "the Toilet Bowl." We could not control what people said about us; we could control, however, what happened on the field.

After Coach Lengyel gave his "Win one for the Gipper" speech, we were fired up. The crowd was cheering loudly, and I couldn't wait to get my first hit. All those hard summer workouts had prepared me for this season opener. We won the coin toss and elected to receive, and Reggie started the game with several good plays. Our drive stalled, and we punted. Coach Riley yelled, "Defense, go hit somebody!" I ran onto the field with every piece of padding the equipment manager had. This the moment I'd been waiting for, a dream fulfilled.

If I hadn't injured my shoulder during the fourth quarter, my dream would have been even more storybook, but my shoulder got banged up. Dr. Craythorn confirmed I'd damaged my deltoid again. I was fearful that I'd lose my starting position. I remembered almost losing an opportunity to play at Steubenville because of an injury. I had made up my mind that the only way I was coming off the field was on a stretcher.

UNKNOWN ILLNESS

My shoulder injury was not my only problem. I was running out of gas every practice, which was unusual for me; stamina was my strong suit. I concluded I'd probably worked out too much prior to summer camp and had run into that proverbial brick wall during the incredibly hot summer. Nevertheless, I practiced every day without complaint. Some teammates asked me, "Are you dieting?" I said, "No way! I'm trying to gain weight." But when I stepped on the scales, I saw I was down to 198, 14 pounds less than when I had arrived at school. What's more, I was falling asleep during class even though I was going to bed at 8:00, and that was strange — I was a night person. I also lost my appetite, but I thought that was due more to the fact I didn't like the cafeteria food and would skip meals. I thought that blocking and tackling the bigger players were wearing me out. As a result, I didn't say anything about my declining health.

My play, however, dropped off enough that I lost my starting position to Freddie Payne, whose starting position I had taken; the defensive end position was one of the most contested positions on the team. I just didn't have my A-game, so I sat, my first time out of the starting lineup in almost three years.

I was getting depressed; my grades were dropping, I couldn't eat or sleep, and I wasn't a starter. From time to time I'd bump heads with the defensive coordinator, an old-school coach who didn't like something about me. He called me "Superfly," probably because I wore a multicolored sweatband. I wasn't trying to be cool, make a fashion statement, or set myself apart from my teammates. I did like dressing up every day in a suit or sport coat and nice slacks and a nice shirt, all color-coordinated. I'd picked up this habit from my father, and it was the case with the majority of men in Steubenville. As I was preparing myself for success, I wanted to look successful. When I bought a classy briefcase to lug my books around, I started a trend on campus and took some credit for boosting the bookstore's sales of the item. Furthermore, I remembered people laughing at me when I was young because of my raggedy clothes, and I never wanted that to happen again. In all due respect to the coach, I was not deliberately trying to be different—my upbringing made me different.

To LIVE OR NOT TO LIVE

I once heard a clinician say that there's a ten-second window that determines whether a person will take someone else's life or his or her own life. Past that ten-second window, there's a greater chance nothing will happen. During 1972, I was in that ten-second window. I was seriously considering suicide because my life seemed to be going backward. The pain in my shoulder was too much to endure, my playing time was diminishing, and my grades were dropping.

I was sitting in my dorm room in a state of hopelessness. I'd entertained the thought of ending my life. Then, for a moment a sense of calm entered into my spirit. Out of the blue, something admonished me to call Nick Diniaco, my former boss, mentor and friend. I told him that I wanted to quit the football team and school because I couldn't deal with my injuries, illnesses, and issues with my defensive coordinator. Unbeknownst to Nick, I was trying to say goodbye. Nick, a man of influence and faith, told me to hang in there, things would get better. "If you quit the team, all of your hard work would have been for nothing, and the coach trying to make things difficult for you wins, so fight for your position. You're are a winner, and we're proud of you."

Diniaco also reminded me that my success in life was not going to be defined whether I could play football or not. He told me, "Don't be so quick to complain about anything, because millions would love to have the good and the bad of your life."

I thought about the promise I made to my mother and the seventy-five plane crash victims, specifically Scottie Reese. Furthermore, I had been raised in a Christian home in which suicide was not acceptable; my pastor and my parents taught me that anyone who committed suicide just bought a one-way ticket to hell. I decided to live.

I learned from my conversation with Nick that life is fragile and never should be taken for granted. I was privileged to be a Marshall University football player and felt an obligation to play through frustration, fatigue, and pain. From that day onward, I've tried to accomplish everything I could that day because tomorrow is never promised. I realized how the Marshall University football players who perished in a plane crash would serve as an inspiration to me for the rest of my life. My work for God was not finished. In Romans 8:26-30, we read,

> Likewise the Spirit also helps in our weaknesses.
> For we do not know what we should pray for as we
> ought, but the Spirit Himself makes intercession for us
> with groaning which cannot be uttered. Now he who
> searches the hearts knows what the mind of the Spirit is,
> because He makes intercession for the saints according
> to the will of God. And we know that all things work
> together for good to those who love God to those who
> are called according to His purpose. For whom He fore
> new, He also predestined to be conformed to the image
> of His son, that He might be the firstborn among many
> brethren. Moreover whom He predestined, these He
> also called; whom He called, these He also justified;
> whom He justified, these He also glorified.

I know someone is always praying for me because God has blessed me abundantly.

CHAPTER TWELVE

HOW THE MARSHALL UNIVERSITY CRASH VICTIMS INSPIRED ME

It was a cool, rainy night clouded by fog and smoke in Ceredo, West Virginia, near West Huntington, on November 14, 1970, when a plane that had left Stallings Field in Kingston, North Carolina, bound for Huntington, West Virginia. As the plane made its final approach, it hit the tops of trees on a hillside and burst into flames. Nobody survived. The nation was shocked by the news, and Marshall University's community was grief stricken. Death had robbed so many talented souls of the opportunity of achieving their potential.

The horrible crash inspired me to play football in honor of Scottie Reese. Besides my wife, Delia, and my son, Brian, no one else knew I'd played the rest of my football career for Scottie until twenty-eight years later. Coach Lengyel and I stayed in contact over the years and got together when Navy played Georgia Tech, a game the coach invited me and my wife to during the 2000 season. Here's my thank you letter to Coach Lengyel.

September 29, 2000
Coach Lengyel
Athletic Director
566 Brownson Road
Annapolis, MD 21402

Dear Coach Lengyel:

I am sorry that it has taken me so long to thank you
and to reflect on our reunion at the Navy — Georgia
Tech game on September 16th. Since my wife and I last
saw you, I have completed a two-week class, a trip to
Ohio to see my oldest sister who is losing her bout with
cancer, and undergoing surgery of my own. It was great
seeing you. You really look good.

Additionally, we enjoyed conversing with the Admiral
and the other nice gentleman including the President of
the Detroit Red Wings in the press box. By the way, I
e-mailed Tom Burbage. He said that he had to miss the
game because he had to attend a board meeting.

To reflect on the past, thanks for awarding me a full
scholarship at Marshall. Although I could have gone
to one of the marquee schools like Notre Dame, Ohio
State, Nebraska, Pittsburgh, Iowa, Iowa State, Illinois,
Indiana, California, Purdue, Minnesota, Syracuse and
others, I'm glad that I chose the green and white colors
of the Thundering Herd. I still love the sound of that
nickname.

You sold me when you said, "a lot of schools want
you, but we need you," I'm glad that I accepted the
challenge to attend Marshall. Moreover, I am blessed
to have forged a lasting relationship with my wife, my
teammates, the alumni and people like the Diniacos.
Last, but not least, your wife and you. My only regret, I
couldn't perform at an optimal level because of my new
debilitating injuries and illnesses. As a result, I felt that

I let the team down, you and Scottie Reese. Yes, Scottie Reese!

As I was walking down Gullickson Hall during my recruiting visit, I paid homage to the players and staff that perished in the plane crash. For some reason, I connected with the spirit of Scottie Reese. Therefore, I wanted to play for him and me. My legendary #84 was not available. Scottie's #83 was gone. So, I selected the hallowed #80. #80 was worn by Dennis "The Menace" Blevins, a fleet-footed and slick wide receiver from Bluefield, West Virginia.

Reggie had informed me that Scottie and I were similar in size, ability, speed and aggression. For that reason, I carried Scottie in my spirit. Actually, I tried to play with a torn deltoid injury and a viral hepatitis illness. Ironically, my bout with hepatitis almost cost me my life. You know it's funny. I had not disclosed my desire to play for Scottie, except to my wife. I had to keep playing in spite of my injuries and illnesses because Scottie was resting. In fact, my body was racked with excruciating pain every day since the first time that I injured it at Ellsworth Community College during the 1971 season. That pain lingered throughout my two years at Marshall and 18 years beyond Marshall. I just wanted to play badly. I almost pulled it off. I can end this chapter of my life. Thank you for believing in my athletic ability.

In addition to that, thanks for creating an avenue of learning. Because of your commitment to academics, I earned three college degrees. Furthermore, I became the model citizen that the Diniacos encouraged me to be. My wife and I started GED program at a local church because it was needed. This was our way of giving back to others. I try to encourage young athletes to excel in the classroom. If the young prospective student-athlete performs in the classroom, I contact small colleges and major universities throughout the country on their behalf. I tried to extend the same amount of patience that you extended me.

In closing, I am forwarding my resume in which I am extremely proud. I always wanted to be able to articulate a sentence to avoid the "dumb athlete" perception. I didn't make all-conference or all-American consideration for Scottie and me. However, we got three degrees.

Again, thanks, Coach. You are truly inspirational.

Les "Praying Mantis" Hicks for Scottie Reese

Because Scottie had made the ultimate sacrifice, I followed suit by sacrificing my talent for the betterment of the team. I played hurt and was willing to play multiple positions including defensive tackle, weighing 212 pounds.

The 1970 Marshall University football plane crash taught me how to treasure each moment and each breath. The loss of thirty-six players and five coaches, twenty-four boosters, five support staff members, and five crew members taught me never to take life for granted. I was privileged to play on the behalf of the deceased players in spite of my pain and frustration. Going forward, I treat each day as if it were my last.

CHAPTER THIRTEEN

DOING WHAT I HAD TO DO

To compete for my starting position, I explored all means necessary to minimize injury, including wearing the shoulder harness to keep my shoulder from popping out. My left shoulder and sometimes the arm became limp and unusable for a few minutes. When the pain dulled, I'd resume play.

I was also unknowingly suffering from hepatitis during the '72 season. I had earned the starting defensive end position for the opener with Morehead State and wanted to keep it even with my shoulder injury, but the defensive coordinator replaced me with Freddie Payne. It was strange, sitting on the sidelines watching someone play in my spot, but I stayed focused and prepared.

As the season progressed, I lost weight and became weaker and weaker. I experienced stomach pain and sensory malfunctions. I noticed my eyes and urine had transformed into a yellow color. By midseason, I was waking up sluggishly and becoming more tired as the hours passed. As a result, I failed kinesiology and fell behind in my other studies. I didn't know what was happening.

My frustration grew as the team lost games. This was the first time I'd been on a losing team. I'd do anything to win except cheat. Although I was aware what steroids could have done for me, I decided that I would never use them, so I played the '73 season with hepatitis and my bad shoulder.

THE GLASS BOWL TRANSFORMED
INTO THE TOILET BOWL

I remember when the team flew to the Glass Bowl in Toledo to play the Toledo Rockets. Some players didn't want to make the traveling squad because they were apprehensive about flying. Those who took the flight were very quiet on the bus to the airport; the crash was on their minds. The two-hour flight felt like a nine-hour flight. When the pilot touched down in Toledo, there were a collective sigh of relief. We were ready to play.

Rain came and went throughout the entire game. As the game went on, we noticed a bad smell, which turned out to be cow and horse manure covered with straw on our sidelines. The smell just got worse as the rain went on. The Toledo team had played one of the most unsportsmanlike pranks I ever experienced. We lost a tight game to Toledo, but we kicked butt on the field.

The highlight of the '72 season was starting the season opener with Morehead State and the Northern Illinois game because Dad and three of my brothers saw me play. In addition to that, Tom Mitchell, one of my Steubenville teammates, was the starting safety for Northern Illinois. Tom, pound for pound was the best athlete that played for Steubenville Big Red. He is one of my best friends.

The team suffered a rash of injuries, so we finished the 1972 season with a 2−9 record. However, there were some bright spots with the emergence of Jon "The Rocket" Lockett, Bobby Crawford, Kelly Sherwood, and Roy Tabb. The veterans, Reggie Oliver, Felix Jordan, Ed Carter, Freddie Payne, Charles Henry, George Jackson, Jack Crabtree, Adam Meadows, Rick Meckstroth, and Chuck Wright made notable contributions. Although we lost veteran leadership when Ed Carter, Felix Jordan, George Jackson, Freddie Payne, and others graduated, the Young Thundering Herd II had hope for the '73 season.

ED CARTER

The now-evangelist Ed Carter had a tremendous effect on my life. This six-two, 230-pound reflection of Hercules was an excellent role model on and off the field. The hard-hitting defensive tackle and offensive guard played hard from whistle to whistle; he was the type of player coaches dream about. He didn't smoke, drink, cuss, or party because he was a Christian who told you about saved lives while living one. From time to time, he told me about God's goodness. I already knew about the Lord, but I had deviated from Him, and Ed was quick to see that. I wasn't a bad person, but I was no saint either. I avoided him for a while because I thought I was too young to give up sex, alcohol, and parties; I thought I could serve the Lord later, so I continued in sin for a while. One summer day in 1975, he told me again about God's goodness, and his testimony pricked my heart, but Satan controlled me until the spring of 1979. Today, I thank God for grace and Ed Carter, who planted the seed of salvation that others watered and that the Spirit of God gave increase to.

Evangelist Carter was the only true Christian I knew. Many students had confessed that they were saved, but they were "thundering," not "lightning." Some students said that Jesus was their Lord and Savior, but the way they led their lives said otherwise. Ed Carter was not a hypocrite, and I could feel his virtue. The only time the team wondered about Carter's walk with God was when food was involved. We said that his motto was "God created chicken so that the preacher could live," Once, when we were playing an away game, the waiter at our hotel restaurant brought out a large tray of fried chicken. "Bring that one right here," he told the waiter. "You guys can get the next one." He actually ate the whole tray of chicken, and no one said anything; we just patiently waited for the next tray.

Evangelist Carter and I are still in touch, discussing and praising God for the great things He does for our families and reminiscing the Young Thundering Herd II playing days. He often reminds me about how he put a "slobber knocker" on Johnnie Lewis, my former roommate and longtime friend. Lewis still denies that Evangelist Carter "rocked" his world. He also reminds me that Jim Wulf, a hard-nosed fullback remembers the slobber knockers I used to rock his world with. Evangelist Carter reported that Wulf said that no one has ever hit him as hard as me.

FELIX "FLIP" JORDAN

Felix "Flip" Jordan was from Blue Ash, Ohio. Flip was the glue that held our defense together; he was like a coach on the field, one of the most cerebral players I've ever played with. If you were out of place, he had a stern but professional way of motivating you to cover your position. Flip, a fierce competitor, never took a play off at practice or in the game, and I took comfort in knowing he was the cornerback behind me.

Flip was a man of few words, but when he spoke, everyone listened. He was also very giving of his time and material things, and he played the game of football with pride and passion. I was blessed to have him as a teammate and a friend.

CONCUSSIONS IN FOOTBALL

Back in the day, when a player received a slobber knocker, nobody made a big deal about it because football was a brutal game. I believe that Dick Butkus, an All Pro and Hall of Fame middle linebacker for the Chicago Bears, likened football to "friendly fighting." I received several hits that would have placed me in the concussion category, and I would almost knock myself out while trying to get the attention of opposing players. I often wonder if the slobber knockers were a contributing cause to my suicide thoughts. I can relate to the NFL players who've committed suicide. There are times when I have severe headaches that keep me in bed.

AFTER THE 1972 SEASON

I tried to eat more to regain weight, so I over indulged at the dinner table during Thanksgiving and Christmas breaks. I also got ultrasound treatments and relentlessly followed an aggressive rehab program. To maintain my stamina, speed, and agility, I played intramural basketball during the off-season. One afternoon, when I was doing weight training, I tried to squat approximately 250 pound weights but dropped them because I was feeling lightheaded and nauseous. The coaching staff took me to Cabell Huntington Hospital and was treated and released after a few hours of tests and extensive evaluations. The ER physician got me an appointment with a gastrointestinal specialist who told me I had hepatitis, a potentially fatal condition. I was shocked but somewhat relieved. Again, I thanked God for allowing me to live.

I underwent medication, injections, and bed rest for several weeks, but I wasn't complaining — I was alive. After my near-death experience, everything paled in comparison, including being the starting defensive end. My first order of business was to stay alive. Next was to get ready for the '73 season.

GETTING READY FOR THE 1973 SEASON

Due to my bout with hepatitis that caused me to be inactive for several months, my anxiety level was at an all-time high, and I was very weak, but I was cleared to play. This was the first time in my football career that I wasn't one of the best-conditioned athletes on the field. I was nervous because this was my last year of football eligibility. I couldn't work out due to my hepatitis, and the disease also made shoulder surgery not an option.

Freddie Payne had graduated, so my competition for the starting defensive end position was John Shimp, Bill Yanossy, Pete Diabo, Bob Compton, and Roy Kinneson. In spite of my long layoff, I was listed as the backup defensive end behind John Shimp at the start of spring practice. Shimp and I had a spirited battle for the starting position throughout spring practice. The practices went well for me, and my swag was coming back. I recall Coach Riley dialing up a stunt during the Green-White game. The stunt required the defensive end to stack behind the defensive tackle, and the defensive end crashed hard to the inside or the outside while the defensive tackle made a hard slant the opposite way. The stunt worked perfectly. As I crashed hard off the tackle's rear end, I had a violent collision with the running back, Grayson Profit. I knocked him back about three or four yards, and it took him a few minutes to get up and walk off the field. The hit was a confidence booster that allowed me to make a strong case for the starting defensive end position. I got stronger during spring practice and regained ten pounds because I was eating and sleeping consistently. I was ready to start the '73 season against Morehead State.

Incidentally, a Green-White game is an inner squad scrimmage that is played with game-like conditions. The coaches equally divide the team into two squads, one squad wears Marshall's home green jerseys and the other squad wears the traveling white jerseys. The purpose of this game is to give the coaching staff and fans an opportunity to evaluate the existing talent pool.

THE END OF AN ERA

During the summer, I repeated the kinesiology class I had failed, worked at nickel plant to set aside some money, and got into superior shape for summer camp. My teammates trickled back to the athletic dorm, Hodges Hall, where I met two new roommates, Andre Heath and Johnnie Lewis. Having Andre as a roommate meant trash talk 24/7. Andre's mouth was like a 7-Eleven, always open.

After we talked about our summers, I chatted with my other teammates until 10:00, bed check. I couldn't sleep; my mind was racing throughout the night. I was motivated to be in the starting lineup. I got only a few hours of sleep that night; my adrenaline level was increasing on team bus to Fairfield Stadium. I got dressed hurriedly I couldn't wait to hit somebody. My first practice went very well. As a result, I played with a lot confidence.

The afternoon practice was very hot; the temperature on the artificial turf was just one degree less than the temperature in hell, but I was ready to go out blazing my last year of college football. As always, the defensive end position was hotly contested, no pun intended. I felt like my old self again, able to get to the quarterback, Reggie Oliver, at will. I feared getting a torn ACL or MCL, so I discouraged the offensive players from blocking me low by questioning their manhood. Fullbacks Bobby "Crunch" Crawford and Jim "Bam Bam" Wulf were up for the challenge. They were the toughest blockers I ever went up against, and I was honored to call them my teammates. Bam Bam used to block me until blood from his nose and face covered my jersey. I could have sacked Reggie in the pocket whenever I wanted, but I didn't want to injure him; he was too important to the team.

I was pursuing a running back, I overextended my left shoulder, injuring it once again. I got it treated with therapy and medicine, but it ached continually. I had to compete injured against some good defensive ends before the season opener. Taking nothing away from those against whom I competed, I would have preferred to have been beaten out by them instead of beaten down by injuries.

THE 1973 SEASON

Coming into the '73 season, I was as tight as clam with lock jaw to relieve the tension, I pledged the Kappa Alpha Psi fraternity with Robert "Crunch" Crawford and Johnnie Lewis, Jr. Pledging Kappa Alpha Psi was a diversion from football. As well, Alpha Kappa Alpha sorority had five girls pledging concurrently with us. Rich Harris, one of my pledge brothers proposed that everyone on our pledge line date our opposite numbers on AKA pledge line. Delia Graham was my opposite number, so my mission was to get a date with her.

LOVE BY THE NUMBERS

Delia, a five-four, 112-pound beauty from Charleston, West Virginia, and I were opposites. She was quiet, unlike me. I was taller by more than a foot and outweighed her by a hundred pounds. She was a homebody while I was constantly on the move. She was conservative, and I was liberal. I met her at a Halloween party that Kappa Alpha Psi fraternity and Alpha Kappa Alpha sorority had forged a partnership to provide food, fun, and games for underprivileged youth off campus. We had a good, casual conversation, but I didn't see her for two months due to football practice and pledging. I will pick up on this story later.

CHAPTER FOURTEEN

THE BLACK GREEK STEP SHOW

On a chilly Friday evening, I was getting ready to serve as emcee for one of the biggest black events at Marshall. I reached deep into my extensive wardrobe and came up with a cream suit with crimson accessories. I was sharp as a double-edged razor; it was showtime. I was live and in color for the annual Marshall University Black Greek Step Show. Steve Turner assisted me with the emcee duties.

The show opened with Alpha Phi Alpha fraternity's steppers, whom I brought on stage. Then it happened. I didn't see it coming. I remember standing on stage and making eye contact with Delia. Her smile changed my life. The glow of her flawless, pecan skin color could have illuminated the gateways to heaven. Her hair was styled perfectly. For those of you who might not know, back in the '70s, (black females and males braided their hair overnight and combed it out in the morning, allowing their hair to expand and create a better style.) Delia's lips were like candy waiting to be enjoyed; she was a dream. Although I was mesmerized, she already had a boyfriend, so I had to hold back the magnetism I felt between us until the day I'd be reborn.

BACK TO FOOTBALL

As we prepared for the opening game, my shoulder started popping out more often than not; my frustration grew because my dream appeared to be slipping away. My football career rested on my oft-injured shoulder. For the first time, I had doubts about playing with my pain, and I felt I was going to let Scottie down, but I was determined to hang in there and not let circumstances defeat me. I'd learned a lot the night I had been contemplating suicide, and the memory of those who had died in the plane crash made me treasure each moment and every breath. I knew I couldn't go forward looking back, and I knew God had blessed me with my abilities for football and studies. I thanked Him for my humble spirit, for giving me the mind to place others ahead of myself and not be selfish. I realized I played football—it didn't play me. I was blessed with the talent to play, and it opened up opportunities I would not have had if I hadn't played, including the degrees I ended up earning, funded by full scholarships. I willed myself by the grace of God to play football even with indescribable pain and also to excel in the classroom. I knew I could do all things through Christ, who strengthened me.

A NEW CHALLENGE

The heavy hitting in practice decimated the ranks of our tight ends, so the coaches asked me to play that position, thinking I could minimize my injuries at this position. However, my shoulder harness kept me from moving my left arm any more than four inches from my side, limiting my ability to catch passes. I remained a defensive end.

We were optimistic about the '73 opener against Morehead. The Young Thundering Herd II's offense and defense had improved substantially over the previous season; The Herd was bigger, stronger, and faster. We ended up 4 — 7; we should have won at least seven games, but we could not overcome costly mistakes. We did beat Morehead, but we lost to Ohio University on Thanksgiving Day.

I made some key plays that season, one of them against Northern Illinois. I made two blocks that let Mark Miller make a game-winning touchdown. I wasn't able to play against Dayton, however, and make up for my subpar '72 game against them.

So there it was. My football career had ended. I was overcome by a vast array of emotions as I cleaned out my locker. Outside, I took a last glance at the empty bleachers that once held our adoring fans. I gazed at the field, which had been my sanctuary. I knew I'd never play on that field again. I thought about the crash victims who'd never gotten the opportunity to reflect on the days gone by, as I was doing. As I drove away, I felt devastated, wishing for one more chance to accomplish all the things I hadn't on the football field.

A NEAR FATAL FLAW AND UNFULFILLED POTENTIAL

When I joined the eclectic group of athletes, the Marshall coaching staff and I had high expectations of me being a difference maker on the grieve-stricken Young Thundering Herd Football Team. Having said that, I'd placed an extraordinary amount of pressure on myself because Steubenville Big Red football players had established a reputation of being difference makers wherever they matriculated. Because I was ill and injured both years at Marshall, my potential was unfulfilled. As a result, I considered my contributions to the Marshall Plan a total failure. I'd based a successful life on athletic accolades in lieu of things off the field.

After playing my last against Ohio University, I backslid into another state of depression. I tried to escape my depression by drinking for extended periods of time. I almost became an alcoholic. When I was in the midst of despair, the Lord said, "That's enough!" My faith in Him allowed me to refrain from my self-destructive ways. I stopped drinking immediately. Then, the Lord placed a hedge around me in the person of Ed Carter.

He gave me the confirmation that Christ was the answer. At that point, I turned my life around.

THE END OF MY COLLEGE CAREER

On my way for a Thanksgiving visit with my family, I was going to enjoy family, food, and friends before going back to Marshall. For the first time, I didn't have to worry about rehabilitating my shoulder, lifting weights, or getting ready for spring and summer practices. However, I entertained those thoughts for just a fleeting moment. I was either a football junkie or a glutton for punishment—I decided to give the NFL a try as a strong safety, will linebacker, or tight end with the Cincinnati Bengals, Pittsburgh Steelers, the then —Boston Patriots, and the then— Houston Oilers.

Because I was preparing for a NFL tryouts, I elected to forgo surgery because I didn't have enough time to heal or go through rehab. I once again got myself in great shape while studying hard to graduate on time.

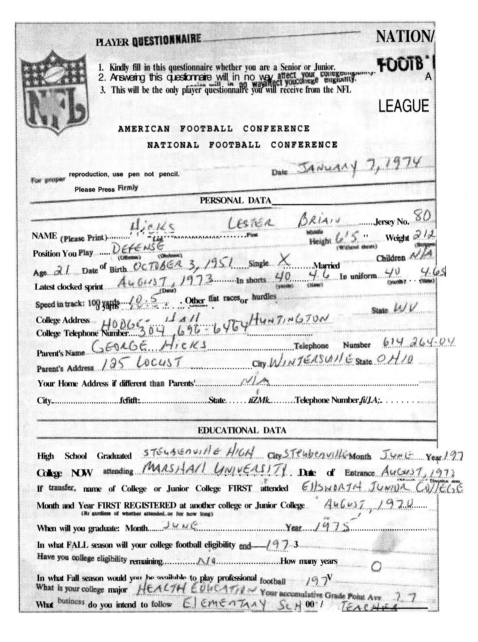

How NATE RUFFIN SUPPORTED ME

Nate Ruffin helped me make my transition from football to the classroom, tutoring me until sometimes as late as 2:00 in the morning. He taught me safety engineering, and he called me "Dress for Les" because he liked the way I dressed. He and his wife, Sharon, had Delia and me stay with them for homecoming weekends. He was a true friend, mentor, confidant, coach, and fraternity brother; I've been blessed to know him.

MY FIRST DATE WITH DELLA

One December night, I walked across campus to the Coffee House, a grill that offered sandwiches and steaks. As I was ordering dinner, I saw Della with two friends. I walked over to her table, asking to join them. We all engaged in conversation until the place closed. When I asked Della if I could walk her back to her dorm, she consented. When we reached her dorm, we talked for just a bit because it was cold, but she did tell me she had broken up with her boyfriend. We start seeing each other on a regular basis, and that's when we learned we were total opposites. In spite of that, we got along very well. Opposites do attract! I stayed on campus that Christmas break, as did Della, whose mother was married to a military man and was in London. She and I dated from 1973 until 1977.

SAD NEWS

Delia and I liked to watch pro football on television. In January of '73, we watched the Miami Dolphins defeat the Washington Redskins in Super Bowl VII in my dorm room. We were enjoying ourselves until I got a call from Nate Freeman, Teddy's older brother. He told me that Teddy's body had been recovered from the Ohio River; he was gone. I had a very hard time processing this bad news. Teddy had told me years earlier that he didn't want to die by drowning. I felt that I had lost a blood brother, but fortunately, Della was there for me.

TEDDY'S HOME GOING

Three days later, I left Huntington on a cold, snowy January morning and arrived in Steubenville a couple of hours before Teddy's home going service. As the family had requested, I did the eulogy, the toughest thing I've done in my life. By the grace of God, I was able to get through it. Ironically, my second eulogy was for my oldest brother, June, who committed suicide in 1983, another emotionally draining time.

If my memory serves me, Bill Ellis was the only member of our basketball team who showed up for Teddy's service. We always called Bill our "blue-eyed brother." We hung out with Bill on and off the court, and he's a true friend I'll always love. This was a very difficult time for me, so if I've omitted a teammate who attended the home going, please accept my apology.

Teddy was destined for greatness, but somewhere, somehow, he'd lost focus. He was an outstanding athlete and my number one friend of friends. Whenever I was in Steubenville, I'd check on Mrs. Freeman, and every time I'd knock on her door, I'd hope I'd awake from a dream and see Teddy answering it. It took me a long time to accept Teddy was gone.

I WANTED A WIN FOR MY FRIEND

After Teddy's home going celebration, I left Steubenville to get back to campus for an intramural basketball championship game at Marshall. At first, my game was off because I was stiff and cold from the long ride, and I was emotionally exhausted as well.

I wanted to win this game in Teddy's honor, but by the time I'd establish some rhythm in the fourth period, the game was over.

After the game, I sat in the bleachers and talked with Jane English. During our discussion, a big football lineman stepped on my coat and struck the back of my head. I asked, "Can't you say excuse me?" He said, "You're in my way," I stood up and hit him with a haymaker followed by three wicked combinations to his head, ending the fight before it had even started. However, I broke my hand when one of my combinations grazed off his head and struck a brick wall. The timing of my injury could not have come at a worse time; I would not be able to try out for the NFL in the spring. I took this as a sign that football beyond college was not in the cards for me.

WALKING AWAY FROM FOOTBALL

I was tired of dealing with pain and rehab. I'd sufferedconcussions, a broken hand, a broken thumb, three broken fingers, cracked ribs, a partially torn deltoid, bruised kidney, sprained ankles and hands, and chipped teeth. You can image how my opponents ended up, but from that day forward, my goal was to be a better student and a better person. To this day, I have never regretted my decision.

After making my decision, I walked away from the game. It had enabled me to play in front of adoring fans; to make lifelong friends of coaches, teammates, and doctors; to earn three degrees; and to learn discipline. I always liked the idea of playing football, but I never liked watching others play.

CLOSING IN ON GRADUATION DAY

Prior to graduation, Dave Graham and I moved into a house off the Marshall campus. Then, I enrolled in graduate school. My employer, Owens-Illinois gave me three blessings. First, O-I paid my way through graduate school. What's more, the company modified my work schedule allowing me to attend classes before or after work. Second, the company placed me in O-I's Safety Intern Program which gave me insight into becoming a safety professional. Last, O-I waived the agreement that would require me to work within the corporation when the first safety job was available. Therefore, I had the option of interviewing with any company where a career opportunity existed for me after graduation.

On May 11, 1975, I earned a Bachelor of Arts degree in Health Education. Then, eighteen months later, I earned a Master of Science degree in Occupational Safety and Industrial Management on December 17, 1976, thus exceeding all expectations of me by far. I'd prevailed against all odds. When I received my master degree, especially, I'd wished that my parents could have shared this incredible moment with me physically. I know that they were there in spirit.

On May 11, 1977, my wife, Della received a Bachelor of Arts degree in Speech Pathology. She served an outstanding support system while I was working towards both degrees. Oftentimes, I'd study at her on campus apartment to get away from distractions that are associated with living in a residential area with many children.

Now that I'd graduated, I was sure that I'd leave West Virginia. That's when Della initiated a conversation about marriage, I heard her but didn't hear her; I was still evaluating the situation. I asked her, "Can you spend the rest of your life living for the Lord?" She said yes. She passed the test; I knew she and I would be compatible. I'd had serious relationships with two other girlfriends who had given me the wrong answer to that question. I wanted to live for the Lord, and I wanted a wife who felt the same way. On December 17, 1977, I asked Della to marry me. There was something about December. Not only did we start dating in December, we got married in December as well.

To save money, we decided against a formal wedding. In fact, we half-eloped and got married December 23, 1977, at the home of my landlord, Lee Ernest McClinton and his wife Audrey. Delia's maid of honor was Yvonne Towns (Roberson), and my best man was Ron Williams. The officiating pastor was the late Reverend Ward. We furnished our home with the money we saved by not having a wedding.

After the wedding, we informed our parents and relatives that we were coming home. We stopped in Charleston, West Virginia; Columbus, Ohio; Detroit; and finally Steubenville, Ohio, during Christmas break. Back at Marshall, we told our friends we were married. Some people couldn't believe how fast our marriage had happened, but that was how Della and I moved.

CHAPTER FIFTEEN

FROM ATHLETE-STUDENT
TO STUDENT-ATHLETE

Dr. Marvin Mills, my professor, confidant, educational advisor, mentor, fraternity brother, and longtime friend helped me decide to further my education. In a poignant conversation, he told me, "Being a NFL football player is a dream very few athletes realize". Dr. Mills emphasized that injuries, luck, and being in the right place at the right time are factors that determine the athlete's fate. He stressed that a college degree was the way to ensure a sustainable livelihood. Mills told me that many companies would be looking for highly qualified safety engineers with master degrees. He said that employers would need skilled safety engineers to interpret the laws imposed by the Occupational Safety and Health Act in 1970. OSHA was a watchdog administration that required all companies employing more than ten people to provide the workers with a safe and healthful work environment. Dr. Mills stressed, "There are no trade secrets in the safety profession. It is an honorable profession that allows a person an opportunity to educate workers about hazardous conditions that could cause injury, even death throughout the workplace." That's why, I decided to obtain my master degree in occupational safety.

I recall being in one of Dr. Mills' graduate school safety classes. He asked us to read a book and present our findings to the class. When it was my turn, I tried to pull a fast one. I pulled excerpts from the front, middle, and end of the book. Dr. Mills had the reputation of being a no-nonsense professor; he knew I had not read the book. He stopped me in the midst of my ramblings. "Hicks, if you don't want to get the full benefit of your grant from Owens-Illinois, drop my class tonight. I'm not going to tolerate anything less than excellence." I was totally embarrassed. Dr. Mills was my fraternity brother. Therefore, Dr. Mills' class was not high on my "to attend list". Consequently, he rode me repeatedly. By remaining in his class, I learned the value of education from Dr. Mills.

Over time, my defining moment was when Dr. Mills asked me to speak to his graduate students at Murray State, a high honor. I owe everything I achieved in the classroom to Dr. Mills, who is almost ninety-two. We talk on the phone at least once a week. I was honored to learn that he calls me one of his sons and has a room reserved in his home for any of my family members, and I have reciprocated that honor. Dr. Mills used to visit me in Atlanta, and he helped me with this book. In fact, he made me promise I'd have it completed before he passed away. Since Dr. Mills transformed me from athlete-student to student-athlete in his class in November 1976, I made a commitment never to disappoint him again. To date, I've kept that promise.

TOMORROW IS NOT PROMISED

I could thank the senior management team at Owens-Illinois for the rest of my life and it probably still might not be enough. Not only did this great company pick up my tab for graduate school, but they allowed me to learn about safety while on the job. When I was not learning about safety, I was packing bottles and working on a furnace rebuild. Life was good until my bubble burst.

I remember the suicide of a fan and a friend. Bill, a mentally challenged coworker at Owens-Illinois, loved to talk about

Marshall football, work, family, life—everything. I remember working the 3:00 PM-11:00 PM shift so I could attend classes during the day. I was in the process of clocking out when Bill stopped me. He wanted to talk; he had something on his mind. I told him I had to drive to Columbus, Ohio to pick up my dad and head to Detroit for Christmas. I was in a hurry, but I apologized to Bill and promised we'd talk after the holiday. I remember him brushing his blond hair from his bright blue eyes.

When I came back to work, I tried to find Bill immediately, but a coworker told me Bill had committed suicide the night I'd left. I was overcome by guilt. If I had taken the time, would he have been alive? I cried throughout the evening. Every time I think about him, I still well up, and I've cried less than seven times in my sixty-one years.

The experience taught me to take the time to listen to anyone who wanted to talk regardless of my schedule; you never know what a person is thinking. If my friend Nick hadn't taken the time to talk to me, I would have killed myself. My grief for Bill continues to this day.

CHAPTER SIXTEEN

WHY I VALUE EDUCATION

I value education because my parents and older siblings were deprived of it. Many of you have probably heard the Black College Foundation's commercial, "A mind is a terrible thing to waste." I add to that, "Knowledge is power." My parents and some siblings were rendered powerless because they were not educated.

The best thing that happened to me was moving to Ohio, where I was able to receive a good education. I tried to earn every degree my parents and siblings were not able to pursue. I began to value education more after Alex Haley's television series Roots and classroom discussions regarding Willie Lynch's The Making of a Slave. Lynch, a British slave owner in the West Indies, offered the following suggestions to his fellow Virginia slave owners.

- Outline the number of differences among slaves and make the differences bigger.
- Use fear, distrust, and envy to control them.
- Use age, color or shade, texture of hair, occupations on the plantation, intelligence, size, sex, sizes of plantations, status on plantations to divide them.
- Prevent the slaves from educating themselves.
- Beat the slaves until they live in fear.
- Train the black male slaves to be mentally weak and dependent but physically strong.
- Train the slaves to love and always be obedient to their masters.

My desire for education increased even more. When I used to hear, "If you want to hide something from a Negro/black person/ n—r, hide it in a book," I'd be insulted, but it would motivate me. I read how the slaves and white instructors were punished for teaching slaves how to read. During the eighteenth century, no school in the South admitted black children; the slave owners feared that black literacy would threaten their slave system. Laws were passed in the South forbidding slaves to read or write or anyone to teach them reading or writing.

- In South Carolina, those who taught slaves were fined up to 100 pounds.
- In North Carolina, teachers were ran out of town for teaching slaves.
- In Norfolk, Virginia, a teacher was imprisoned for teaching slaves.
- Death could be the punishment for teaching a slave to read.

Slave owners feared slave rebellions and escapes, so they limited their slaves' contact with the outside world to eliminate their dreams and aspirations, keep them from learning about slave rebellions, and stifle their mental faculties.

- Virginia punished violations of laws prohibiting teaching slaves with twenty lashes to the slave and a $100 fine to the teacher.
- In Kentucky, education of slaves was legal but almost nonexistent.

Lynch's teachings certainly affected my family. My father was born in the late 1890s, and my mother was born in the early 1900s; they were affected by the no-education rule imposed on my ancestors. My parents and some of my siblings were forced to pick cotton, fruits, and vegetables from when they were only six or seven.

Nonetheless, I didn't value education when I was young. I'd not study much and just try to cram for exams. As a result, my grades weren't good enough to get me into a major college without going to a junior college first.

I understand why my parents could not educate themselves. However, when we moved to Ohio, my siblings and I had an opportunity to get an education. Some of us were able to take advantage of that. I thank God for giving me the determination to value education; my education enabled me to change the course of my life.

DIVISIVENESS BETWEEN FRATERNITIES AND SORORITIES IN COLLEGE

Today, Willie Lynch's teachings still affect blacks; not enough of them have capitalized on the opportunity to educate themselves. Even those who have gone to college are victims of Lynch's ideas about creating divisiveness among black people. Some go to predominantly black colleges, while others face adversity at predominantly white universities. I'm just the messenger here. I ask every black Greek to search his or her heart and recognize that disliking brothers or sisters because of the color of their fraternity or sorority shirts is shameful behavior; we're all the same color underneath our crimson/cream, purple/gold, pink/green, red/white, and blue/white T-shirts. I have a method to unite black Greeks. All black Greek organizations should:

- Establish on-campus corporations to increase their purchasing power and increase Greek and non-Greek attendance at concerts, parties, various events, etc., and share the proceeds.
- Formulate a large group of black Greeks to assist the elderly by cutting grass, shoveling snow — whatever our elderly need.

* Create Big Brother and Big Sister programs to help the young who could benefit from positive role models. Promote achievement in their communities by tutoring those in need.

* Support other black Greek organizations while remaining true to the fraternities and sororities to which they have given their hearts.

CHAPTER SEVENTEEN

WHY I CHOSE SAFETY ENGINEERING
FOR MY PROFESSION

My initial interest in workplace safety started while I was working at Weirton Steel Mill in Weirton, West Virginia. The company's safety representative would present weekly safety talks, and that got me thinking about working as a safety representative. Dr. Mills, head of the safety department at Marshall, closed the deal by selling me on safety engineering as a career. I chose the field because it held no trade secrets; it was a humanistic way of extending godly love to those hard working employees who needed to avoid accidents in order to provide for their families. I considered safety engineering a ministry; good safety engineers are present and accountable all the time, and they focus on building relationships, training people—even if that requires scolding them—being good listeners, and keeping their promises.

I was also on a personal crusade; my father had lost an eye on the job. I knew others who had been seriously injured on the job, even some who had died on the job. I made a commitment to do all I could to prevent serious injury or death on my watch.

Dr. Mills taught me to spend most of my time on the production floor to create the "halo effect"; workers are more likely to follow safety rules if they know the safety engineer can pop up at any time. Over my thirty-five years in the profession, I've learned that workers don't do what you expect, so you have to inspect. I believe I was born to be a safety engineer. As a result,

I earned a master of science degree in occupational safety and industrial management, made possible by Owen-Illinois paying for graduate school.

I made it a habit to get to work before the start of a shift to meet and greet employees in a nonthreatening atmosphere; it was my way of letting them know I cared about their families and them. I consistently enforced all safety rules because I knew an accident could cause debilitating injuries or even death. I always wanted to minimize if not eliminate the possibility of injury.

CHAPTER EIGHTEEN

LIFE IN SOUTH CAROLINA

After I received my master degree in 1976, I landed a job with the Louis Rich Company in Newberry, South Carolina. My task was to implement the company's first formal safety program. My wife stayed in Huntington for a while, until school was out. We were separated newlyweds who spent a lot of time on the phone.

A PROMISE FULFILLED

In April 1977, my sister called with the news that a drug dealer had mistakenly shot up my father's house, almost hitting him and others inside. Della and I agreed it was time to bring Dad to South Carolina, and surprisingly, Dad agreed to the move. I drove to Columbus immediately, and we were back in South Carolina the next day. I had mixed emotions when we arrived in Columbia. I felt good because I had fulfilled the promise to take care of Dad and was pleased to get him out of harm's way in Columbus, but I sensed he'd be homesick.

Della and I treated Dad like a king because he was worthy of it. I assumed responsibility for the chores and cooking until Della finished her teaching obligation in Kentucky. Dad and I rented a U-Haul to bring her to South Carolina. This was the first time we were together as a family.

Things were somewhat awkward at first because Della and I were newlyweds, and she didn't know my dad that well. I had a long commute to my job because there was no housing near it, and I also put in very long hours. I'd leave the house around 5:00 in the morning and would not get back until 8:00 at night. As a result, Della was spending more time with my dad than I was. Turns out, I didn't have to worry about that; they got along very well because of their humble, quiet demeanors.

One evening, Dad asked me to buy him some medication for his corns. When I pulled his sock off to apply it, I noticed his little toe had darkened and was full of pus. It had rotted so much that I could have pulled it off. He told me he'd tried to remove his corns with a double-edged razor and had cut his toe, which had gotten infected. To compound the problem, Dad was a diabetic, which slowed any healing. Della and I took him to the emergency room, and the doctor there referred Dad to an orthopedic doctor.

Because Dad had given me power of attorney, I made decisions on his behalf. The first decision was to give authorization for the removal of Dad's little toe, but then the infection and problem spread, and he had to have his leg amputated below the knee and then above the knee. Each decision was gut wrenching, but I had to make them. Dad didn't understand what was going on; he was not used to seeing doctors, especially for surgery. Dad was prepped for surgery two times on the same day, but because he was a Medicaid patient, his surgery got delayed because of some affluent patients going to the front of the line. After a couple of delays, Dad went under the knife. After three-quarters of his right leg had been amputated, he was delirious because he had been given several doses of medication. He pulled a collection device off his stump and threw it against the wall. He was high as Mount Everest.

TOUGH LOVE

The doctor told me to ensure Dad adhered to a strict diet and a rigorous rehabilitation regime because he had to be fitted for a prosthetic leg in about six weeks. The doctor told me I'd have to exercise tough love while rehabbing my Dad's stump. Although it was very difficult for me to put Dad on a diet and make him work out every day, I followed the doctor's orders.

Dad didn't like being on a diet, so he found a way around it. Dad had befriended our elderly neighbors and had convinced them that Della and I were starving him. As a result, the neighbors used to give him food all day. After three weeks, we noticed that Dad was gaining weight against his doctor's orders, and we couldn't understand that. One day, however, I emptied the garbage and saw scraps of food we hadn't prepared. We finally learned that Dad had been playing us. We had a polite discussion with our neighbors about Dad's strict diet. Although they told us they'd stop giving Dad food, I suspected they had a backup plan, because Dad didn't lose any weight.

As well, he found a way to bamboozle Della about exercising. She eventually told me that he was cheating on his exercises every day. Della said he entertained her just about every day with the guitar and harmonica and relaxed all day. When he heard me pulling into the driveway, he'd tell Della, "Here come that boy. I better get up and do my exercises." As I'd walk through the door, I would hear him counting out loud, "Eighty-nine, ninety, ninety-one," as if he had started at one. Dad was as sly as a fox, and we'd argue about his playing me big time.

When Dad would tell me that his amputated toe was itching, I thought he was losing his mind. I learned from the doctor that the nerve ending in Dad's stump still existed even though his leg was gone, and it sent signals that his toe itched. This is called "phantom pain," which amputees can suffer from. I thought I had heard it all.

Dad and I had a debate about his getting a prosthetic leg. He said, "If God wanted me to walk, he wouldn't have taken my leg in the first place." He said it was his time to rest. I sensed Dad was longing to be around the rest of the family. He loved being around his children and grandchildren back home, and all his favorite foods were on a no-go list because of his condition. What's more, I worked a lot. All these things lefthim longing for home. My primary goal was to make him happy, and I realized I was being selfish by having him stay with me. I asked him where he really wanted to be, and he said Detroit. He told us we had treated him well, but he was homesick. Della and I packed his belongings and took him to Detroit. In my heart, I know I had treated him with respect, and I hoped he was as proud of me as I was of him.

OUR FIRST BORN—A GIRL!

On March 24, 1979, we were blessed with LeShea Dionne Hicks. Her birth solidified our marriage and brought us closer to God. The birth of LeShea also taught us unconditional love; whether we were feeding her, changing her diapers, or bathing her, we always got a big smile from her. That was all LeShea had to give, but she gave it over and over, and she gave us joy beyond imagination.

After Shea's christening, we decided to bring her up in the church, so we started attending every Sunday. She would have been the joy of my dad's life if she had been born a year earlier, but that was not meant to be. I remember the first time she was going to be out of our presence. We agreed to allow Delia's mother, Shirley, to keep her for a week. When Shirley and her husband, Baz, drove away with LeShea, we saw her bright eyes peering through the back window. Della started crying as though she would never see her again. I was sad too, of course, but I reminded Delia that Shea was going only for a week, not a lifetime.

MY WORK

I was the safety coordinator at Louis Rich, a turkey processing plant in Newberry, South Carolina from 1978 to 1979. It was a non-union company that employed over 800 workers who processed 17,000 turkeys daily. My biggest task was to create a strong culture of safety at a company that had not had a formal safety program, so I was given the latitude to set one up. The workers were primarily females. In addition to the predominantly female workforce, the company employed twenty mentally challenged migrant workers to remove the live turkeys from a continuing flow of eighteen-wheelers and put them on rotating shackles. To get a feel for the industry and the workers, I worked most of the jobs throughout the plant. As the turkeys moved through the "kill room," two skilled workers in yellow slicker suits cut the turkeys' jugular veins. This was the most critical part of the process; if the workers failed to cut the jugular vein in the right spot, the turkeys would turn blue and would have to be discarded. I didn't work in the kill room because precision at this task was critical.

The turkeys then went through a water room where their feathers were removed, and the next step was the evisceration line. Workers there would use their hands to remove the turkeys' entrails and send them on for other workers for dissection. The workers wielded razor-sharp knives in hands protected by wire-mesh gloves. One worker suffered a severe hand injury when she tried to catch her falling knife with an ungloved hand and cut several ligaments, a permanent disability. I felt bad for the worker; she was a good employee and a single parent who needed the income. As well, she was LeShea's babysitter.

Unfortunately, we had several amputations because some employees failed to follow safety rules. I used to keep a bucket of ice water in my office to help preserve limbs in the event of an amputation.

Speaking of my office, I didn't really have one. I shared a room inside the processing facility with five supervisors. There was nowhere to hang pictures, degrees, or certifications because the processing area had to be slightly above freezing and there were streams of water running down the walls constantly. We had to wear sweaters under our lab coats to keep warm.

After I worked most of the job classifications, I set up a job safety analysis program. A job safety analysis analyzes each step in job task to identify potential hazards. The work I had done on the lines allowed me to identify not only the potential hazards but also which employees were safety conscious, and that information told me who the risk takers were. In addition to the job task analysis, I implemented the following safety programs at Louis Rich:

- Formal safety meetings
- Job observations
- Personal protective equipment
- Rules, regulations, and practices
- Job procedures and practices
- Skills training
- Emergency preparedness, including a fire brigade
- Inspections

I also had to supervise the cooks, the knife room attendants, the truck drivers, and the sewing room workers, and I did this all working up to seventy hours a week with no overtime pay.

The reason for my long commute to work was that most of the homes near work were trailer homes. Once, my wife heard about a home for rent in the area, and we were very excited about seeing the house. We called the landlord to inquire about the vacant house immediately. When we got there to see it, a large, vicious dog charged us. Della and I got back in our car just before the dog got to us. A tall, red-haired gentleman with a mouth full of chewing tobacco walked up and asked, "What do you folks want around here?" I told him my wife had just called about the house for rent. The old man responded, "I just rented it about five minutes ago." Before we drove off, I asked the old man if his dog bit. He said, "Sometimes he will, sometimes he won't." That was the final straw. We opted to live in Columbia, South Carolina, even with the sixty-five mile commute it meant for me.

As a young safety engineer fresh out of graduate school, I found myself not practicing what I preached; I got a speeding ticket in my first month in South Carolina and lost my driver's license. Fortunately, my wife worked in Newberry before LeShea was born, so I could hitch rides with her. When she was on pregnancy leave, Columbia experienced a rare ice storm that broke some branches off a pecan tree near our bedroom. They crashed through the window and landed about a foot from our heads. They could have killed us, but we were blessed; we got out of bed unscathed.

Due to my driving irresponsibility, I was on the verge of losing my job with my first child on the way and a sixty-five-mile commute. I didn't know what to do. Then God blessed me miraculously by placing Johnnie Miller, one of the plant workers, in my life. I hardly knew Johnnie, but he drove me from Newberry to Columbia every day for two months. Johnnie was one of the best friends I've ever had. Even after I left Louis Rich, he and I stayed in contact. I still recognize Johnnie as family.

My next position was as safety and fire protection supervisor at Hooker Chemical, an elemental phosphorus manufacturing plant in Columbia, Tennessee that employed 350 employees. I came into a much better situation at Hooker, a subsidiary of Occidental Petroleum with a very respectable safety record. A lot of attention was given to safety guidelines because errors could have been catastrophic.

I landed in a good place; my manager, Eddie Floyd, taught me a lot about safety when it came to handling elemental phosphorus, which could not come in contact with water or oxygen. To minimize the volatile reaction of the phosphorus, it had to be covered with sand, dirt, and or water to keep it from igniting. Processing phosphorus required numerous conveyors. It was first heated in a furnace to about 3,000 degrees until it was molten, and then it was poured into molds that were formed in the sand. Every now and then, water would get into the molten metal and it caused an explosion that could rock the city and lead you to believe you were under attack. During my tenure there, I Implemented a safety incentive program, reduced the rate of incidents by 25 percent, and reduced the number of lost workdays by 20 percent.

One time, I saw a worker step into a sump that contained a considerable amount of phosphorus residue. When he pulled himself out, he caught fire when oxygen ignited the phosphorus, and he ran off. Several supervisory personnel and workers caught up to him and rolled him on the ground, wrapping him in a Kevlar blanket to eliminate the oxygen. When they got him to the hospital and removed the Kevlar blanket, the phosphorous reignited. As he was flailing his arms, some of the residue shook loose and burned my cheek. The young worker, just nineteen, suffered third-degree burns from the waist down and lost his genitals, but he survived.

On a lighter side, I remember when we conducted a fire drill. The alarm went off, and everyone had to evacuate the building. I was responsible for checking the main office building to ensure we had 100 percent evacuation. As I was walking down the hallway, a female office worker dashed out of the restroom and ran past me hurriedly, trailing a six-foot stream of toilet paper from her pants. Much to her chagrin, over 500 of her coworkers witnessed her embarrassing moment as well.

After almost two years at Hooker Chemical, I accepted a position with Olin Corporation in Augusta, Georgia, where I worked from 1981 to 1982. They had made me an offer I just couldn't refuse. The company gave me a considerable raise and assistance with purchasing our first brand-new home. My official job title was manager, safety and loss prevention. Olin had one of the best safety records in the chemical industry. The plant processed chlorine and caustic soda and employed just under 200. The mercury that the company used in some of its processes posed serious health issues, and that's where I came in. While there, I implemented a fire brigade, improved the off-the-job safety program, and decreased the rate of accidents by 33 percent.

Because chemical plants were dangerous, I insisted that all safety rules were strictly adhered to. I recall one morning hearing a big explosion right after I had completed my daily inspection. The rest of the management team and I investigated the incident and found out that an after cooler had malfunctioned. If I had been in the area just half an hour earlier, I would have lost my life. I thanked God for protecting me that morning.

Just before I took the job with Olin, I happened to meet the late James Brown, the R&B icon, on a flight. Apparently, Mr. Brown loved country ham; his entourage was carrying eight of them back to Augusta. As I was boarding, Mr. Brown spoke to me, asking if I lived in Augusta. I told him I lived in Tennessee and had a job interview with Olin. As if I didn't already know, he told me he was an Augusta native and said it was a great place to live. If I needed any assistance, he told me, I was to give him a call. I was surprised when he gave me his telephone number.

After I got the job with Olin, Della, LeShea and I arrived in Augusta, I called Mr. Brown and spoke to his office manager. I explained how he and I had met at the airport. She transferred my call to him, and he remembered me. He asked me where I was staying because he was going to have one of his employees pick me up. I told him that wouldn't be necessary because Olin had already found me a home. I thanked him for his willingness to help my family and me, and I hung up in disbelief. James Brown was truly a great person who sincerely wanted to help me. Most stars would not have given me a minute of their time. I'll never forget his kind gesture, and I pray that his seed and his seed's seed be blessed of the Lord.

I decided I didn't like the managerial side of the safety profession because I didn't like sitting in an office all day. I knew I'd be more of an asset to a company and its workers by spending most of my time on the floor, in the trenches, so to speak.

My job at Olin was the first job that required me to travel, and I did so about 35 percent of my time. Being an introvert, I didn't like meeting new people all the time, so Olin and I parted ways. Olin picked up the tab for me to meet with Drake, Beam and Morin, a top-notch job search company in Atlanta, and Olin paid my salary until I found employment with Gulfstream Aerospace, where I worked from 1982 to 1984.

Gulfstream Aerospace, a corporate jet manufacturer in Savannah, Georgia, employed over 1,500. It brought me in to succeed a retiring manager of safety. Gulfstream was the cleanest, largest facility I ever worked for. My primary responsibilities were conducting daily inspections, training supervisors and managers on safety principles, conducting surveys, and chairing safety committee meetings. While I was there, I launched a campaign that reduced all accidents by 25 percent, streamlined annual accident incident rate from 6.55 to 4.76, and sliced $300,000 off my company's Workers Compensation costs in fifteen months.

While employed with Gulfstream, I experienced many high points, including the birth of our one and only son, Brian, a closer walk with God, and substantial growth as a safety professional. The low points included but were not limited to, the passing of my father, the excessive fungus in Savannah that caused heath issues for me and my children, and my children getting their first taste of racism. They couldn't understand why they couldn't play with their white friends when their friends' grandparents were around or when their parents had company over. The parents would tell our children to stay away until their guests left. These antics infuriated Della and me, and the parents got a piece of my mind.

I experienced a near-death experience in Savannah. As I was on my way home one day, a tornado touched down twenty-five yards in front of me while I was crossing a bridge. My heart almost stopped—I thought I was going to wind up in the Atlantic Ocean.

EMPLOYEES SAY THE DARNDEST THINGS

I was fasting one day, and that made by breath foul. I was having a Bible discussion with one of the janitors during the morning break. He asked me, "Do you want a stick of gum?" I said no, and our conversation continued. He kept on offering gum, but I kept on refusing. "Les," he finally said emphatically, "in the name of Jesus please take this gum. "Your breath is really stinking," I did the bad-breath check, blowing into my cuffed hands and sniffing, and he was right. I wasn't mad at him at all; I respected him for telling me. Most people wouldn't have done what he had. If you smell something, say something!

CHAPTER NINETEEN

ON THE MOVE AGAIN

When I worked for Hooker Chemical, we lived in Columbia, Tennessee, the exact opposite of Columbia, South Carolina. The majority of the work with Hooker was on the outside, and majority of my work at Louis Rich had been inside. We got a lot of snow in Columbia, Tennessee, and hardly any in Columbia, South Carolina. Hooker's employees were union and the majority were male, whereas Louis Rich didn't have a union, and most of the employees were female. Columbia, Tennessee, had fewer than 30,000 residents, while Columbia, South Carolina, had close to 130,000.

We enjoyed a lot of spiritual growth while living in Columbia, Tennessee. At first, Della and I joined the Church of God, which had about 100 members, most of whom were elderly. Delia and I "adopted" an elderly couple in their eighties. The husband was blind, and the wife was very sickly. Delia cooked meals, washed clothes, and cleaned house for them as needed while I cut the grass and shoveled snow for them. Even when we left this church, we maintained a close relationship with them.

We later joined the Church of God in Christ, a denomination with which I was familiar; my mother had joined that church after we relocated from Georgia. The Church of God in Christ had a pastor in his late seventies who lived in Nashville, Tennessee, about sixty-seven miles north of Columbia. The church membership consisted of his son, his grandson, an elderly lady, her daughter, and three small children. The pastor had converted a small house into a church.

I served as janitor, grass cutter, and fire starter. The first time I cut the grass in the backyard, it was so high I had to use a swing blade, and I prayed relentlessly that a snake wouldn't bite me. I made sure that the restrooms were sparkling, I shoveled snow, and I fired up the wood-burning stove on cold days a few hours before service.

ZEAL WITHOUT WISDOM

The Bible instructs us to study ourselves to be approved. As young converts, my wife and I were overzealous regarding Romans 2:7: "Consider what I say, and may the Lord give you understanding in all things." On occasion, some preachers preach their own personal faiths, philosophies, or beliefs. Pastor Cain was an old school preacher who believed in faith healing without the aid of medication. Before I was able to understand the Word of God for myself, I relied heavily on what I received from the pulpit. As a result, I had a root canal without anesthesia. My wife thought I'd lost my mind by enduring such pain, but God protects fools and babies. By faith, I was blessed to suffer through that painful ordeal. Pastor Cain was a true man of God who lived by his conviction, and I learned from this experience and grew from it.

Although Columbia, Tennessee, was a nice place to live, we decided to relocate for personal and professional reasons. Della felt badly because her skills in speech pathology didn't seem to be helping the special-needs students; they showed little progress from year to year. As for me, I really liked my job, but I was used to living in a larger city, so that's when I hired on with Olin. In spite of the promotion and salary increase, our decision to relocate was very difficult because we'd grown accustomed to the elderly couple and Pastor Cain.

LIFE IN AUGUSTA, GEORGIA

We made a very smooth transition to Augusta. During our first week there, we bought a new home. One of my Olin coworkers told me about a church conference that would give Della and me an excellent opportunity to evaluate churches and their pastors. Five churches attended a conference, and we liked one. After the service was over, everyone exchanged pleasantries. Delia and I tried to shake each pastor's hand, hoping to learn more about their churches, but one of the pastors gave us a slight snub. Later that night, however, he stopped by our hotel room to apologize for not giving us more attention at the service. He'd heard that I was a new safety manager at Olin, and he invited us to attend his church, saying he had a position for me. We decided against this church immediately because I sensed this pastor was more interested in tithing and prestige. I had a big position with a high salary for someone my age, and Della was a professional speech pathologist. I was not into titles, and I was turned off by the fact that I'd been offered a position in the church without any background check. I could have been a thief, a pedophile, or a murderer.

We finally chose a church in Thompson, Georgia, headed by Mark Walden, a very humble pastor. Our former pastor, Pastor Cain, drove down to Augusta to see what type of church we had selected. He attended our church services, had a long visit with Pastor Walden, and gave us his approval.

I remember carrying out a safety assignment on the railroad tracks inside Olin's property line. I had high boots on because rattlesnakes had been spotted there, and I saw two. The only weapon I had was a flashlight, which I shone in their eyes while yelling. The snakes slithered away, perhaps saving me from a heart attack or bite.

I thought Olin would be my final destination. However, Augusta was not the place for us. That was when I took the position at Gulfstream in Savannah. The company's safety manager was retiring shortly, and I was hired to step into that position. I left Gulfstream two years later, however, because the humidity in the area caused ear infections, and I was tired of battling sand gnats. My headhunter presented me with two opportunities, Boeing, in Renton, Washington, and Lockheed Martin, in Marietta, Georgia. I chose Lockheed over Boeing because it rained a little too much for me in Washington.

THE DEATH OF MY FATHER

Dad had survived heart attacks, strokes, and diabetes, but he succumbed to gangrene while living in Detroit with my sister Mary on December 8, 1983. He suffered badly for about a week. He refused to eat, but he drank a little coffee. I believe my grief-stricken Dad had longed to be with my mother. I was at work when my sister informed me of Dad's passing. Due to the reports that I'd been receiving from my sister, I knew the word could come without a moment's notice. I was hoping for a miracle that never happened. A man who had meant so much to me had departed this life. He was an old oak tree with an eagle trapped inside. Society, like the landowners back in Georgia, saw him as a worthless person on his way to nowhere. However, he soared magnificently in spite of those who disrespected him.

I had lost both my parents. Dad had worked hard his whole life. He never owned much, but he was rich in work ethic, integrity, character, the ability to be a great father, and all the other key components. Specifically, I remember when Dad was beaten and spat on when he confronted a landowner about bilking him out of his wages. Although there were twenty mouths to feed, we always had something to eat. He never hit my mother, and he worked hard picking cotton, fruit, and vegetables. He even dug graves with a pick and shovel for extra money all through the night.

I inherited my work ethic from him and passed it on to my children, LeShea, Brian, Tiffany, and Shante'. I feel like a multimillionaire because of all the inherited principles Dad instilled in me; he was my hero.

I thank God for allowing me to wake up every morning and play the hand that's dealt me the way Mom and Dad would have played it.

DAD'S HOME GOING

Dad's home going service was held on a quiet, cold, Detroit day. There were not many mourners other than family, but that was because the majority of Dad's siblings in Reynolds and friends back in Steubenville were too feeble or had already passed away; Dad himself was close to ninety and hadn't made that many friends in Detroit.

Although my father couldn't read or write, he had a master degree in life survival skills and another one in family commitment. Back during my college days, it was rare to meet a black athlete who had both parents in his life. Many of my black teammates said their fathers had abandoned their families, and others said that their mothers had been abused by their fathers, but my father always treated my mother as the queen she was, and that set an example for me.

I'm not a shadow of the man my father was; he had set that bar high, but I always tried to reach it. I've been a good provider. My family has always had food and a comfortable place to live. However, I didn't try to give my children everything they requested; I wanted them to earn things. I taught them to give their employers an honest day's work for an honest day's pay so they could feel good about what they did and what they earned. They took on paper routes and learned discipline and responsibility. They earned company awards for perfect attendance and zero customer complaints. Three of my four children have graduated college, and they did so in the top third of their classes, with honors.

I am still trying to put my arms around all the infinite wisdom my father shared with me. I had lost a role model, a confidante, and a hero. I did not shed any tears because I was very respectful of my parents. I gave them expressions of my love when they were alive. I was not a saint, but I never caused my parents any trouble because I honored them.

OUR LOVE FOR THE ELDERLY

I have always been drawn to elderly people; our elderly friends always outnumbered our younger friends. I like the elderly because they genuinely appreciate friendship, and they've always given Della and me fresh perspectives on life with no unnecessary drama. Some of our younger friends like to keep up with the Joneses, gossip, and other things that didn't set well with us, which just isn't us. For the most part, we have chosen to be loners.

THE BIRTH OF OUR NUMBER-ONE SON

On December 29, 1984, Della gave birth to Brian, who will carry on the family name. He was a very alert baby who was always into something, and I loved the idea of having another man around the house.

Although we relocated to Savannah, Della and I decided to attend church in Augusta because I didn't like changing some things. So, we drove from Savannah to Augusta every weekend. To defray our costs, Pastor Walden made arrangements for us to stay with two church members. Because we were not comfortable with those arrangements for personal reasons, Pastor Walden suggested we stay in his home during the weekends, and we did so until we moved to Powder Springs, Georgia.

BUILDING A LIFE AT LOCKHEED

From 1984 to the present, I've worked at Lockheed Martin in Marietta. Lockheed manufactures cargo planes and fighter jets and has employed as many as 21,000. I've worked as a safety engineer, human resources representative, quality circle facilitator, recreation coordinator, and pollution prevention coordinator. These are among my accomplishments for this company:

2008-2012
- Implemented a Hazard Recognition Program
- Launched a daily Inspection Safety Compliance Program
- Ensured all OSHA-regulated machines were compliant with OSHA regulations
- Investigated incidents in a timely manner with sound corrective action ideas
- Reemphasized the value of safety control zones
- Implemented "100+ Days Without an Accident" Incentive Program
- Launched a "Voice for Choice" Personal Protective Equipment (PPE) Selection Program

2000-2008
- Earned twenty-one awards from Georgia's regulatory agencies, including two PACE Awards from the Clean Air Campaign
- Coordinated a Recycling Incentive Program

- Made several presentations at Fulton and Paulding Counties
- Received a first-place award for an anti-litter program
- Implemented an "Adopt A Mile" program
- Increased car and vanpool ridership markedly
- Recycled 79 percent of all nonhazardous waste
- Received a third-place award for the "Best Recycling Program in the State of Georgia"

1990-2000

- Served as acting Safety Engineer Lead
- Made 1,433 OSHA-regulated machines compliant
- Increased safety awareness by educating employees on the spot
- Lauded by corporate auditors for preparation of the OSHA How-To Manual

1986-1990

- Served as Quality Circle Facilitator for forty-three quality circles
- Generated cost savings by implementing employee ideas saving millions in cost avoidance

1986-1990

- Resolved employee-related issues based on company policies and procedures
- Advised department management on salaried employee complaints and issues
- Handled sensitive information in a confidential manner
- Reviewed and approved authorizing paperwork affecting the status of salaried personnel to ensure conformance with these policies

1986-1990

- Planned all company recreational activities and social events
- Organized and collected carts for "Food for the Needy" Program
- Ensured that store inventory was accurate
- Maintained hobby club areas
- Organized golf tournaments and other sporting events

1984-1986

- Conducted inspections with the United States Air Force to ensure plant-wide compliance
- Provided innovative ideas to reduce accidents and save money

I've always taken pride in Lockheed's slogan, "Never Forget Who You Are Working For." When I started in '84, I had to prove myself. One morning, my supervisor asked me to conduct a lower explosive limit (LEL) reading to determine the amount of dangerous gases or vapors inside the aircraft wings that could affect the worker or workplace safety. The probe attached to the meter I was using to measure the air inside the wing fell off, right into the wing and out of reach. Retrieving it was going to require the removal of a panel on the wing and would slow down the production process. Although no one had seen me drop the probe, fear and embarrassment gripped me. I could have easily covered my mistake up, but I read a sign: "FOD Kills," and "FOD" stands for "foreign object damage or debris." Another sign read, "A Mistake Covered Up May Cause the Death of a Brave Pilot." I reported my mistake to the supervisor for that aircraft and my own supervisor.

Truth set me free. Word got around about my responsible decision, and I was recognized for my integrity. I was asked to tell my story in The Lockheed Signature, a video that dealt with ethics. What's more, I was selected to represent Lockheed Martin in promotional ads and a recycling video I had conceived. I was featured in the Atlanta Business Chronicle for two PACE Awards. Recently, I was recognized by Janet Nash, Vice-President, C-130J Program and Earl Pinkett, Safety Manager, C-130J Program in a Lockheed Martin newsletter for my accomplishments for changing the program's safety culture. I was overwhelmed and humbled by this gesture, the greatest honor bestowed on me during my thirty-five years as a safety professional. Because of God's favor, I know that if you don't seek glory, glory will find you. I don't have enough room on my wall to hang all the awards, certificates, and memorabilia I've received.

Treena, a coworker, knew I had an association with John McVay, vice president of the San Francisco 49ers, who had once tried to get me to come to Dayton University while he was serving as head football coach. Treena, a huge 49ers fan, asked me if I could get her son, Clay, autographed pictures of Joe Montana, Jerry Rice, and Roger Craig. McVay promptly mailed me the autographed pictures for Clay and the following letter.

Vice President
San Francisco 49ers

March 20, 1990

Lester Hicks
3288 Apache Court
Powder Springs, Georgia 30073

Dear Les:

Thank you for your letter of March 15. It was nice to hear that things are going well for you and that you have four wonderful kids.

We will send the pictures you requested.

Best wishes to you and your family.

Sincerely,
John McVay

Atlanta Business Chronicle 2007 Pace Awards
Lockheed encourages commuting alternatives
By Tonya Layman

Can employees who are under union agreement successfully take part in a company-sponsored commute alternatives program? Officials at Lockheed Martin Aeronautics Co. in Marietta say yes.

Because a majority of Lockheed's workers are under union agreement, it knew it was facing a challenge when it set a goal of establishing carpool and vanpool programs and implementing compressed workweeks. But after the union accepted the programs, employees embraced it. More than 1,300 signed up for the rideshare program, making it the largest sign-up total at a single site in the state. The vanpool program operates at least 60 vans that get preferential parking at the 1,000-acre plant.

Even bigger than vanpooling at Lockheed is compressed workweek scheduling. This program eliminates 6,700 vehicles from metro Atlanta roads one day every other week. All employees work a nine-day, 80-hour two-week work cycle. It is the one program that all employees can participate in.

"Lockheed Martin Aeronautics Co. promotes commuting alternative programs as a way to support the community by reducing traffic congestion, improving air quality by giving its workforce an extra 24 days off the highways per year," said Les Hicks, Lockheed's pollution prevention coordinator. "This environment, ultimately resulting in an improved work-life balance. From a personal benefit, the compressed workweek allows each employee to save vacation time and reduce the cost of commuting."

The company has reduced vehicle trips annually by 301,500 and has documented it has reduced more than 4 million vehicle miles each year.

"Some specific benefits we've realized are improved morale, reduced overall operating expense, reduce parking both on the part of the employee and company," Hicks said.

Due to its success with these programs, Lockheed has received the PACE Spotlight Award. But it isn't stopping there. It is exploring new commute options and operations programs that include replacing on-site, gas-powered fleet vehicles with electric ones.

In 2001, Lockheed signed on as a partner of The Clean Air Campaign. Since then it has served as an advocate for the organization. It participated as guest on the 2007 Alternative Work Schedule Lunch and Learn panel to help other employers implement semi-created a case study for the Clean Air Campaign to use when marketing to other employers throughout the region.

"Lockheed had to get their union on board to make the compressed workweek happen. With 6,700 employees now working a 9/80, they are great example of what can be accomplished," said Kevin Green, executive director of the Clean Air Campaign.

Lockheed also offers a customized Commuter Rewards Web and a Guaranteed Ride Home Program. It recently rolled out a Going Green Pre-Tax Incentive Program to reward its employees for commute program.

Lockheed Martin Aeronautics
Number of employees: 6,700
Commute alternatives offered: Compressed workweek, vanpooling, carpooling, bicycling, walking, pre-tax program and transit

How It's working: The commute options are working because Lockheed Martin Aeronautics is committed to minimizing commute-related problems, showing dedication to helping employees with commuting challenges, and reducing traffic congestion and poor air quality in the community.

Programs take off successfully: Les Hicks of Lockheed says the company and its workers benefit from the efforts to cut down on vehicle miles traveled each year.

Reprinted with permission of the Atlanta Business
Chronicle

InSite

Representatives from LM AERO—Marietta
Environmental, Safety and Health accepted two
awards from the Keep Georgia Beautiful Organization.
LM AERO—Marietta received a First Place Award for the
coordination and promotion of the Ga. Governor's Anti-
Litter Campaign. The Marietta facility was recognized for
being the first Georgia Company to embrace the Keep
Georgia Beautiful mission which is to build and sustain
community and environmental activities and behaviors
resulting in a more beautiful Georgia.

The second award was for having the third best Non-
Hazardous Waste Recycling Program in the State
of Georgia. The Marietta facility was recognized
for educating employees through employee training
sessions, a web site that contains information about the
facility's comprehensive recycling programs, newsletter
articles, and training videos and presentations on
collection containers.

Photo by John Rossino

InSite

Incidentally ... Employee Dedicates Time Mentoring Children

Les Hicks, a pollution prevention coordinator in Marietta, was known around college campuses in the Ohio Valley for some of the punishment he delivered as a defensive end on the football field. Now, Les hits the books instead of opposing ball carriers as a counselor for young student athletes.

"Most athletes need to know that is important to be a good student first," Les says. "What happens off the playing field is what counts. To succeed, you have to take care of business in the classroom."

Highly recruited by major colleges throughout the country, Les decided to attend Marshall after the school lost its football team and coaching staff in a tragic crash in late 1970.

"I wanted to help a team that was struggling," Les says. "A lot of the other college football programs wanted me, but the coach at Marshall told me that he needed me." That's what sold me on the school and how I live my life today. My commitment to students is to lead by example."

Through referrals and by word-of-mouth, Les, who received both his undergraduate and master degrees from Marshall, spends countless hours every month in the inner city working with athletes. Les teaches his pupils, ranging from 6 to 18 of all races, how to lead better lives, or just how to survive another day in today's ever changing world.

"Most of the kids I work with are from single parent households," Les says. "They need a father figure to help

213

them with the basics . .. proper dress, grooming, language and good study habits. The rewards for me have been endless. I'm just glad to be able to make a difference."

Reprinted with permission of Lockheed Martin Community Relations.

Lockheed—Georgia Interdepartmental Communication
Subject: Corporate Ethics Video
November 10, 1988

Corporate Public Relations is going to do a new ethics video, "The Lockheed Signature," featuring Dan Tellup. A crew will be going around to various companies conducting interviews. They want to talk to some enthusiastic people who would like to talk about job quality, teamwork, company and employee responsibility, etc.

I have selected three names of people who would probably best serve the needs of the video requirements. The following are employed in your areas:

Ralph Peterson (Fanto)
Les Hicks (Rainwater)
Devina Henderson (Wilson)

While the taping is not scheduled to occur until the
week of November 28th, I would like to talk to these
individuals about the video and have at least one dry
run. I would envision about an hour of preparation and
one hour during the actual shooting of the tape.

If you agree to letting these individuals participate, I
would appreciate having you notify them and call me at
Ext. 3211 when they have the opportunity.

Thanks,
Dick

Reprinted with permission of Lockheed Martin
Community Relations

I have always liked the idea of being the unsung hero. I chose
safety engineering because I love the profession. My goal is and
always has been to protect workers from themselves.

During my tenure at Lockheed Martin, my wife gave birth to our
last two daughters, Tiffany and Shanté. After their births, I had
to focus my attention on protecting them as well.

TIFFANY AND SHANTÉ

Tiffany and Shanté were born while I was at Lockheed Martin.
Tiffany, our third, was born prematurely. She was a fun-loving
baby who always stayed very close to us. Shanté, our last, was a
low-maintenance, quiet baby and a great blessing.

CHAPTER TWENTY

LISTENING TO THE VOICE WITHIN

I believe all of us have voices inside that compel us to do right or wrong. The right voice is God's, and the wrong voice is Satan's—we have to choose our master. Psalm 84:11 tells us, "For the Lord God is sun and shield; The Lord will give grace and glory; No good thing, He will withhold from those who walk uprightly." In Peter 4:8, we learn that love covers a multitude of sins, and we also know that we are not above temptation. Consider Romans 7:19-25.

For the good that will do, I do not do; but the evil I will not do, that I practice. Now if I do what I do not want to do, it is no longer I who do it, but sin that dwells in me. I find in a law, that evil is present with me, the one who wills to do good. For I delight in the law of God according to the inward man. But I see another law in my members, warring against law of my mind, and bringing me into captivity of the law of sin which is in my members. O wretched man that I am who deliver me from the body of death? I thank God through Jesus Christ our Lord. So, then, with the mind I myself serve of the law of God, but with me the flesh law of sin.

WALKING THROUGH THE VALLEY
IN THE SHADOW OF DEATH

One time, when I was driving to visit my sister Rosetta, who was ill, I looked into my rearview mirror and saw two people drag racing. Ahead, the right lane had been blocked off by concrete barriers for construction purposes, but the drag racer right behind me was coming on strong. Somehow I was able to maneuver around the concrete barriers in the nick of time, narrowly avoiding death one more time. My nerves were shattered for the rest of the trip. Considering all my near-death experiences, I thank God for extending my life time and time again.

During that same trip, I learned on the radio that a tornado was approaching, so I pulled under a bridge and braced myself for the worst. The tornado miraculously veered to the left right before it got to me. As I continued on my journey, I saw overturned semis, damaged houses, and blown-down trees. Can you believe how jittery I was when I arrived in Columbus? Fortunately, Rosetta recovered from her illness.

On top of all that, when I headed home, I had to avoid a semi that had spun out of control, and that made me jumpy for the rest of my journey, afraid of any big truck. The interstate is no place for tentative drivers; they can cause accidents. I had an uncontrollable fear of driving on interstate for many years after that.

THE RIGHT PLACE AT THE WRONG TIME

Delia, LeShea, Brian, Tiffany, Shanté, and I were once on a ten-day family tour with stops in Michigan, Ohio, and West Virginia. We planned to visit Rosetta in Columbus on the fourth leg of the trip. While we were inside her house visiting with her, someone who was trying to park his car hit my new car and bumped it up on the curb, and in Columbus, the curbs are high. I wasn't too upset. My biggest concern was if the car was drivable. I never get worked up over material things. I have things — things don't have me. The driver who hit my car, however, was nervous. I thought he was going to bolt. I told him I'd call the police, but he offered me cash to fix my car, but it was a very low amount. When I turned to get a pen from the glove compartment, a voice

warned me, "Don't do that." I listened. I memorized the drivers'
license plate and called the police.

Afterward, I thanked God for that voice I heard. My wife told me
the driver had had a gun in the back of his pants, and it looked to
her as if he'd been ready to pull it, thinking I was going for a gun
in the glove compartment and could have claimed self-defense.

After the police left, the driver, who turned out to be one of the
biggest drug dealers in Columbus, started talking trash to me. He
vowed to kill my family and I because I could have gotten him
busted. He was serious, but I knew the prayers of the righteous
were covering me.

I called my brother, Willie to let him know that we were coming
over to his house to spend the rest of the night. When we arrived at
his house his lights were out. We knocked on his door very loudly
for approximately five minutes; however, he didn't hear us. By now,
it was too late to check into a hotel. So, we decided to drive across
town to stay with my sister, Ola. We asked Ola if we could spend
the night. She apologetically declined our request. She said that she
was having some issues and that we couldn't spend the night. God
delivered us from out of the hands of the enemy. I didn't realize
that everything happen for a reason that night. We discovered that
the drug dealer knew where Willie and Ola lived. As a result, he'd
intended to exact revenge not only against my family, but against
Willie's and Ola's families as well. God is good and faithful. I glorify
Him for protecting us from unforeseen danger.

On our way to Delia's mom's house in Charleston, WV, we were both
tired, having been through that ordeal with the drug dealer. A state
trooper pulled us over; Della had been weaving all over the highway,
and the trooper thought she was driving under the influence. We
explained our situation, and he let us go with the stipulation that we
get adequate sleep before attempting to get on the road again.

THE GREAT ESCAPE

On one cool, dark April night in 2006, I was driving under the speed limit. Suddenly, I hit a disabled vehicle that had stalled in the middle of the road. This was the first collision that I'd been involved in. I thought my car was about to catch fire, so I struggled through the airbags and got out on the passenger side, as the driver's door was stuck. It took all my strength to push open the damaged passenger door, but I finally got out. Shortly after that, a little Chevy Cavalier hit my car from behind and leapfrogged over my car, hitting the car I had hit. Once again, I thanked God for saving my life. If I had gotten out on the driver's side, or worse, if I had not been able to get out of my car, I could have easily died. The airbags had been released, and my gas tank had been full.

As it turned out, the car I hit had a bad alternator, so it had no lights, and the driver who hit us had been exceeding the speed limit. Those who gathered around the crash scene couldn't believe I had survived. I went to the emergency room for a cut on my forehead and torn back muscles, but the other drivers hadn't suffered any injuries.

A couple of days later, I picked up the police report. The young Jamaican girl, whose car I had hit, had not been cited because her car had been disabled, and she wasn't able to push it off the road. I wasn't cited because I hadn't seen her car. And the third driver wasn't cited because the Jamaican girl's car and my car had been in the road. My attorney told me that the third driver should have been cited for all three accidents, but he pointed out the obvious: I may have lost my car but I was still alive and well. I had escaped the death Angel once again.

These pictures show the near-fatal automobile accident that I was involved in during April.

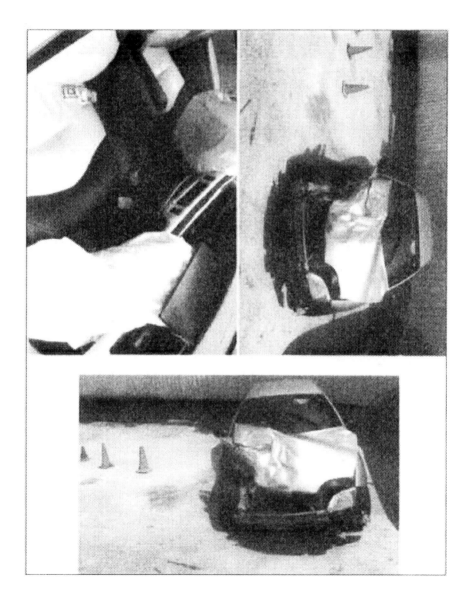

HARD TO STOMACH

I recall getting off work on Monday night, June 26, 2006. My stomach started growling and aching after I ate a sandwich. It got bigger all week long, and I was in such pain that I didn't go to work. I tried everything—Tums, pain meds, hot-water soaks — but nothing worked. By the time I got to my doctor, I looked eight months pregnant. My doctor said he was perplexed because my pain was on the bottom left side of my stomach, not where appendixes are. He sent me to an emergency room, where I had to wait in intense pain for five hours.

The emergency room attendant gave me a barium test so my insides would show up on an X-ray. While I was waiting for my test results, the patient on the other side of my curtain passed away, and this distracted the emergency room attendant, who did not get back to me for hours.

Turns out my appendix had burst as the nurses were taking me to the operating room. The doctor performed emergency surgery on me told me that I was a very lucky man; if I'd not been in the hospital, gangrene could have taken my life, as it had my dad's. When he asked how I had endured so much pain for six days, I told him my pain threshold was high.

They had to drain the poison from my insides through a little hole in my lower stomach, and I had to endure a diet of potato soup, tomato soup, and cranberry juice. I had gas, and I was constipated. My butt was so tight you couldn't have stuck a straight pin in its crack. Some ginger tea fixed all that, but as I was heading for the bathroom for my first bowel movement in ten days, I slipped and tore a muscle near my stomach. On top of that, my massive bowel movement tore up my rectum and left me bleeding. I believe that the massive bowel that I moved was equivalent to a baby. Morphine eased my pain but caused me to hallucinate and talk to every dead person I'd ever known. I saw walls melting, and I was definitely tripping without my luggage. Several coworkers and my boss, Roger Lee, visited me in the hospital, but I was so out of it I didn't realize they were there.

After I got home, I found that bowel movements were unbearable. I scheduled an appointment with the doctor because I couldn't take the pain any longer. He saw my torn-up rectum, but he told me he was going to be out of the office for two weeks and couldn't fix it until he returned. I was so upset that I forgot to pick up the prescription from the office, and due to the prescription's strength, he couldn't call it in. The doctor told me avoid fruits and vegetables that had high acid content.

To avoid the pain, I ate a minimum amount of food to limit my bowel movements, but the pain was unendurable. For the first time in their lives, Della and my kids saw me crying. The pain was severe every time I moved, coughed, or sneezed. One day, I considered taking my life, but then a voice reminded me that I'd go to hell, that my wife and kids would suffer, and I'd let down so many other people. I listened to the voice within and elected to live with my pain.

ALMOST A DEAD AIM

On a cool summer morning in 2007, while I was driving to work, I heard a gunshot and saw a bullet blaze across the road just in front of me. I don't know if it was accidental or intentional, but I knew once again that I was blessed. If I had been driving a little faster, I could have been a statistic.

CHAPTER TWENTY-ONE

BY HIS STRIPES WE ARE HEALED

In 1992, I'd noticed symptoms that gave me an indication that my health was declining. Over time, these symptoms became problematic requiring eight different surgical procedures involving all my major organs. At present, God has healed me of a debilitating illness that has either claimed the lives and/or disabled three of my siblings and several friends. However, God continues to keep His protective shield around me. Moreover, cancer knocks on my door repeatedly, but God refuses to let it completely ravish my body.

I'm blessed because my employer, Lockheed Martin Aeronautics Company has provided my family with outstanding health benefits that has enabled me to afford highly skilled physicians to address our medical issues.

ONLY THE STRONG SURVIVE: IF YOU
THINK YOU CAN, YOU WILL

All in all, I survived my physical difficulties. God has allowed me to persevere my entire life. Nothing has ever been easy for me, but I learned to adjust to whatever trials came my way. The power of life and death is on our tongue. If we speak blessings upon our lives, we will attain them, but if we speak negative things, more often not, the results will be negative. When some people discover they have cancer, they become consumed in self-pity and give up on life. My wife, on the other hand, is a two-time cancer survivor who kept the faith and a smile on her face every day. The joy of the Lord was our strength.

God has given us the ability to believe. If you believe God, success will follow, thus allowing you to overcome all your mistakes. There is power in what we believe. When I received God's Word, everything else became incidental; I knew God was working on my behalf, and this allowed me to accomplished things beyond my wildest dreams and against all odds.

Although no one in my family advocated education, I self-taught myself because I wanted to end the curse of poverty. I was determined to graduate from high school and possibly go to college. After I'd enrolled in college, I remember suffering through physical pain while I studied, and I always focused on earning the degrees I have earned.

After my mother passed away, I became a recluse for almost one year. I overcame my fear of dead people and transferred the anger inside to aggressive play on the football field. Playing with a chip on my shoulder ironically made me a better football player.

In 1986, the first night we were in our house in Powder Springs, Georgia, rains came and flooded the first floor, and our dream house became a nightmare. We suffered a lot of property damage not covered by insurance because it was an act of God. Later, we discovered that the walls were cracking, and an engineer told us our house had been built over a dried creek. We had to have our house jacked up permanently. What's more, we learned the air conditioning and heating units were undersized and had to be replaced.

In 1987, my wife had her first battle with cancer. It would have gone undetected had she not been pregnant with Shanté, our youngest. Because she was preoccupied with her battle with cancer and the pregnancy, she failed her teacher's certification test by one point and lost her job. As a result, I took part-time work as a house painter, working loss prevention for Sears, selling suits and alarm systems, and working as a loan officer. I worked that last job right after work Monday through Thursday and occasionally on Saturdays. I thank Mr. C for giving me an opportunity to work at his company; he was someone else who believed in excellence. Cassandra Kinsey, an extraordinary person, taught me loan solicitation. She also trained me how to close a refinancing deal. If a loan was not in the best interest of elderly borrowers, however, I'd advise them not to, as I didn't want to receive commissions for loans I knew they would probably default on it—that just wouldn't have been fair to anyone no matter how badly we needed the money.

In spite of being unemployed, pregnant, and with cancer, my wife remained upbeat; her faith never wavered. After she gave birth, her cancer was successfully treated and she passed her teacher certification test. Everything worked out.

In 1988, my cousin, Kevin Burks was killed by a group of racists who simply wanted to kill a nigger because they had nothing better to do. Here's what the newspaper wrote.

Martin Jury Studies Case
By Mark Law
Herald-Star Staff Writer
Friday, September 30

STEUBENVILLE—The jury in the Peter L. Martin trial deliberated for almost three hours Thursday afternoon before deciding to quit for the evening and continue deliberations at 9 a.m. today.

The 12-member jury, including the four alternates, is being sequestered by Common Pleas Judge Dominick

Olivito until deliberations are completed. Closing arguments began at 11:30 a.m. Thursday.

Martin is charged with aggravated murder with death penalty specifications, kidnapping and aggravated robbery. Each charge has a firearm specification. David Hudson, 25, and Billy Wayne Smith, 18, both of RD 1, Hammondsville, were indicted on the same charges as Martin. Robert Carpenter, 25, of East Liverpool has pleaded guilty to murder, aggravated robbery and kidnapping as part of a negotiated plea agreement with the prosecutor's office. Carpenter testified in Martin's trial.

Assistant Prosecutor Bruce Dondzilla told the jury Martin, who is one of four people charged with the shooting and stabbing death of Kevin Burks in November, had the intent from the beginning to kill a black man, Dondzilla said Martin was a principal offender in the case. He said witnesses in the case corroborated the defense's claim in the case.

Dondzilla said the four defendants did not take Burks to a city street under a street light because they might have been seen. He said the defendants took Burks to a remote area on Brush Creek Road because they had agreed it would be a good place to hide the body. He told the jury Martin wanted a turn at shooting Burks and shot Burks behind the ear, sending the bullet into Burks's brain.

"The man with the plan is Peter Martin," Dondzilla said. He said Martin was the defendant that came up with the "master plan" to lure Burks into the car and "fininshed the master plan with a bullet to the brain."

Court-appointed defense counsel Samuel Pate told the jury there was reasonable doubt in the case. He said Martin's intoxicated state the night of the killing is no excuse for what happened. He said in Martin's mental condition he could not have formulated the intent to kill Burks from the beginning. "It was more spur-of-the-moment decision-making," Pate said.

Pate told the jury it was Hudson who was the principal offender in the case. He said Martin did not act with prior calculation and design and purpose. He said Burks was dead when Martin took $6 and Food Stamps from Burks's wallet. He said Martin did not intend to cause serious physical harm because Martin had fired only one shot at Burks.

Pate said it was Hudson who deceived Burks into coming with the defendants.

Prosecutor Stephen Stern also addressed the jury saying, "You must find the truth. For if you don't, then what is our hope for justice?"

He said the defendants got tired of shooting up cars and got bored with stealing truck tires. "They decided to kill a human being for the fun of it," Stern said.

Stern said Martin pronounced a death sentence on Burks when he pulled the keys from the ignition as Burks sat in the front attempting to get away from the men.

Stern told the jury the "tragic flaw" in Martin's defense is that he waited nine months to tell anyone he was under the influence of drugs and alcohol. Stern said Martin still had the presence of mind to attempt to cover up the evidence after the incident.

Olivito's instructions to the jury lasted 75 minutes and the jury was given a copy of the instructions for use during deliberations.

Maximum Sentence Received By Martin
By Martin Law
Herald-Star Staff Writer

STEUBENVILLE—Peter L. Martin, 24, received
the maximum sentence allowed by law Friday from
Common Pleas Judge Dominick Olivito for his part in
the Nov. 16 shooting and stabbing death of Kevin Burks
of East Liverpool.

Martin stood with his "hands" in his pockets as Olivito
read the sentences. Martin was convicted of aggravated
murder, with a specification of purposely causing the
death of Burks while committing kidnapping. The jury
did not return with a death penalty recommendation
but did recommend Martin be sentenced to life in prison
with eligibility for parole after 30 years on that charge.
Martin also was convicted of kidnapping and aggravated
robbery. Each charge had a firearm specification.

Olivito first sentenced Martin to serve nine years
(three, three-year consecutive sentences) on the firearm
specifications. The judge then ordered Martin to serve
10 to 25 years on the aggravated robbery charge and
then to serve 10 to 25 years on the kidnapping charge.
Olivito then ordered Martin to serve life in prison on
the aggravated murder charge, with parole eligibility
after 30 years. The sentences are all consecutive to each
other. The first time Martin will be eligible for parole
will be in 50 years or when he is 83 years old.

Defense counsel objected to the consecutive sentences
on the firearm specifications, but Olivita overruled the
objection. Olivito advised Martin of his appeal rights.
Court-appointed defense attorneys Frederic Naragon
and Samuel Pate asked Olivito to appoint two other
attorneys to represent Martin in the appeal process.

Jeanette Hicks, Burks's mother, gave a statement in open court, as allowed by law.

"As a representative for the Kevin Burks family, I feel that I have a right and a duty as a mother to come forth at this time and let the people in the surrounding areas know how our family feels about the verdict that was reached in the Martin case.

"With the jury being an all-white jury, I knew deep down in my heart that they were going to be prejudiced and very biased when it came to this case," she said.

Mrs. Hicks said that anyone who is a human being and looked at the photographs of her son could realize that no matter what color of the skin, he did not deserve to die like he did.

"He begged and pleaded for his life. But was his life spared? No. In your eyes and in the eyes of the jury, killing Kevin was just killing another 'nigger. Did the jury ever consider the feelings of Kevin's family ... evidently not? Kevin had two younger sisters and an 87-year-old grandmother who raised him and looked up to him. But of course, once again, this was not taken into consideration.

"We get up every morning and say 'Hey, Kevin,' but of course Kevin cannot speak back to us because these are pictures . . . the only thing that we have left of Kevin.

"If Peter Martin had not suggested that 'I know a nigger we can get,' my son would still be alive today. No one else even thought of Kevin except Pete, but of course the jury did not take that into consideration either. Kevin may have been black but he wasn't a nigger. Kevin was loved by a lot of people and he loved a lot of people. The one thing my son didn't do was judge people by the color of their skin."

In 1990, when my wife picked up our two-year-old Shanté at her daycare, Della noticed she had a bite that appeared to be developing a small blister that started to change colors. I had to leave town for business, so Della made a doctor's appointment for Shanté the next day. However, Della called me later that day with the news that Shanté had a high fever that led to convulsions. Fortunately, we lived close to the hospital, and Shanté was rushed to the emergency room. We learned she had been bitten by a brown recluse spider and could have died if she had not gotten to the hospital.

In 1992, I lived through another potential tragedy. I was walking to my car one day when it caught on fire. Within minutes, it burned down to the ground. The fire department determined that my fuel line had broken and that the hot engine had ignited the gas. To make matters worse, the insurance company lowball me, so we had to dip into our savings for another car.

On July 3, 1999, my wife called to tell me that Shante' had seen a big snake near our front steps. I was in a meeting when she called, so I told her to call the police. She responded, "What is the police going to do, arrest it?" I laughed, but then I thought of John Brown, a true friend and neighbor who lived just up the street. He came over and killed the snake.

At that time, we had our house on the market for sale. Our realtor called to say she had sold the house, and we were excited. However, our joy was short-lived, because just then it started to rain very hard. In less than an hour, ten feet of water filled our yard and four feet covered the first level of the house. We saw lawn furniture and garbage cans floating all around the house. The weatherman called the storm a hundred-year rain. Unfortunately, the news media reported that our house had flooded because it was the lowest-sitting house in our subdivision. It was build beside a stream running through the subdivision. Our house wasn't going to sell being in now a flood zone.

Once again, we called John for assistance. He was like a State Farm insurance agent—a good neighbor who was always there. He brought squeegees and wet vacuums, and we got to work. We were amazed that Brian, who had been lying in bed watching the NBA draft, wasn't electrocuted by the electrical cords lying in water on the floor in his bedroom.

To our surprise, the water receded as quickly as it came, but I hurt my leg when a mirror fell on it, and the cut became infected because the water was contaminated. John and I worked throughout the night, nonetheless, and improved the house significantly.

The next day, our realtor told us the couple still wanted to see our house, and they came by a couple of hours later. They agreed to buy the house when we knocked $10,000 off our asking price and threw in a weight-training system for their son, a top football prospect for McEachern High School. The only thing they wanted repaired was a light fixture, which ended up costing me only $5.89.

We could have taken advantage of this couple, but we did the right thing. On our own, we painted the outside of the house and the first level after we hired a company to draw the water out of the sheetrock, and we replaced the carpeting. Our net profit on that place was $280, but we ended up feeling good because we had done the right thing.

Ten days later, we moved to our new home. We selected it because it was the highest setting house in our new subdivision.

We were blessed to get a small interest loan from FEMA, and Lockheed Martin gave me a nice donation to help us get back on our feet. My coworkers in the safety department collected money for me as well. My boss, Roger Lee, and a coworker, Errol Clarkston, went out of their way to assist us after our disaster.

Not only did our neighbor John Brown assist us throughout the restoration process, he was also always our go-to guy for car repairs no matter the weather, and he'd never charge us. He braved the heat in our attic—140 degrees in the summer—to fix our air conditioning. Again, he's a rare friend who is always there for us, and I've tried to be the same for him.

In 2000, my wife had another battle with cancer, but she kept her composure before and after surgery, and she's been in remission from both her bouts with cancer.

In 2002, my best friend, Reynard Horston, was involved in a car accident that left him permanently paralyzed. He was T-boned by a fast-moving semi but remained conscious throughout his ordeal. A helicopter took him to Grant Hospital in Columbus, Ohio. While he was there, news came that his sister, who had been battling breast cancer (he was returning home from a visit with her when he'd been hit) had passed away. When he came out of surgery and asked about Stephanie, no one said anything. The doctors instructed his family not to disclose Stephanie's passing; they feared the news could cause Reynard to have a stroke or a heart attack.

Reynard has inspired me tremendously. In spite of his paralysis, he's very productive. In fact, he accomplishes more lying on his back than many able-bodied people do standing up. Reynard has never complained about his tragic accident; instead, he helps others. So, Tino Jackson launched a campaign to have others help Reynard to purchase a van to make his doctor visits easier. Roosevelt "Roe" Andrews, Ricardo Suggs, Bill and Theresa Danaher, Bernie Battistel, Al and Barbara Provenzano, Greg and Andrea Bahen, Willie "Red" and Carolyn Simmons assist Reynard's wife Debbie plus his nephew, Antoine Brown, with his daily care and transportation to the doctor office, church, and sporting events. The Steubenville Herald Star published this article.

Meet the pastor: Quinn welcomes Church sermon topics
Fundraising effort makes van presentation possible
January 15, 2011
The Herald Star

The Christian Brotherhood of Second Baptist Church in Steubenville recently spearheaded efforts to purchase and donate a wheelchair-equipped van to lifelong city resident and fellow church member Reynard "Nardy" Horston.

It took less than a month to make it happen for the Steubenville resident who was paralyzed from the waist down in a traffic accident that occurred approximately seven years ago while he was on his way home from Columbus. The accident occurred two days after his sister, Stephanie Horston, lost her battle to cancer. He had journeyed there to be at her side.

"We were inspired by others doing basically the same thing — people responding to a need," said a group spokesman in explaining how the fundraiser took root toward November's end, resulting in the van being presented during a special church service on Dec. 19 by the Rev. Calvin McLoyd, Jr.

"There are so many good people doing good things in our community. We were compelled by the Holy Spirit to move forward. However, it was not just the Christian Brotherhood. Horston's family, friends, fraternity brothers, past coaches and teammates from Big Red and Marshall University and others who made contributions and made this effort's success," the spokesman said.

The presentation of the van was followed by a reception in the church fellowship hall where an album of cards and letters from contributors was presented to Horston, who expressed his gratitude.

After graduating from Steubenville High School, Horston accepted a scholarship to play football for Marshall University. He was a member of the 1970 freshman team that saw 75 of its varsity football team perish in the plane crash that a recent movie called We Are Marshall documented.

During his freshman year at Marshall, Horston pledged Kappa Alpha Psi fraternity. His dean of pledges was Nate Ruffin, one of the main characters in the movie and one of only four surviving members of the ill-fated varsity team. He and two others were left behind in Huntington, W.Va., because of injuries while a fourth missed the flight.

The effort to raise money came from many directions, including from area football coaches; from childhood friend and fellow fraternity member William Sizemore Jr. organizing help from the KAPPAs; and from Lester Hicks recruiting support from football alumni friends at both Big Red and Marshall.

"It was just unreal," observed Deacon Valentine C. Jackson of the Christian Brotherhood of the response to the fundraiser. "It was very emotional, and it was really nice."

Reprinted with permission of the Steubenville Herald Star.

In 2007, Brian severely tore his knee while descending the stairwell at work. His doctor, a highly regarded orthopedic surgeon on the Atlanta Hawks staff, said it was one of the worst tears he'd seen. However, because of the excellent medical care and a great rehabilitation program, Brian was able to go back to work after a few months.

In 2008, Brian was rushed to the emergency room with chest pains, and we learned that he had a considerable amount of blockage around his heart that required attention. He survived, but a former Georgia Tech basketball star and a member of the Atlanta Hawks passed away due to similar complications.

One time, in 2008, Della started vomiting when she tried to get out of bed. She complained of headaches and dizziness as well, and I actually had to carry her to the car to get to the emergency room. It turned out that she had a severe case of vertigo and could have suffered a stroke. The doctor recommended a nursing home for her while she was recuperating, but I told him that wasn't an option. I took medical leave for several weeks and handled the cooking and cleaning as well as rehabilitating her until she recovered.

In 2008, my sister Darlene lost her long battle with cancer; she had been like a mother to me. I'd moved in with her and her husband, Jerry, after Mama passed. She handled her cancer with dignity. Toward the end, she denied chemo and medication because she didn't feel the need for it. She went quietly during the early morning. I owe everything that I have attained in life to "Doll," Jerry, and the Diniacos. I don't know where I would have ended up without their support. They gave me the motivation and the will to live, and I love life because of their inspiration.

In 2010, Della had extensive back surgery. Ironically, when Della left the hospital for home, she seemed to be in better condition than I was. I stayed in the hospital until she was discharged, sleeping on a short cot that made me (6'5", 245 pounds) sleep in a fetal position. As a result, my back locked up, but I had to fight through the pain because she needed me. It was like the blind leading the blind—we were a pitiful sight, but, like always, we got through by toughness and the prayers of our pastor, Frederick Anderson, and our fellow church members. The complications with her back forced her into early retirement.

WE ARE MARSHALL: THE MOVIE WAS NOT EXACTLY A TRUE STORY

I saw the We Are Marshall movie, which moved me, but I knew several scenes were not accurate and some characters were fictional. I certified this through discussions with teammates, coaches, deceased players' girlfriends, fans, and boosters.

Scene that was Hollywood scripted: The character portrayed by actor Ian McShane and the cheerleader named "Katie" were fictional, as was the star running back, Chris Griffin. Actually, Marshall's top running backs were Joe Hood and Art Harris.

Nate Ruffin did not have a roommate, Tom, who overslept in the Hollywood version. Tom had missed the team plane, and his guilt took away his passion to play football for the Thundering Herd.

Scene that was Hollywood scripted: The Marshall cheerleaders and the marching band did not travel with the team to East Carolina because the school had a losing tradition, so its football program had not been a moneymaker, making it too expensive to fly them along with the team.

Scene that was Hollywood scripted: Coach Red Dawson did not give his seat up to another assistant coach, Deke Brackett. Coach Dawson had made plans to recruit an outstanding junior college prospect who was attending Ferrum Community College in Virginia. A graduate assistant, Gail Parker, gave coach Brackett his seat and accompanied Coach Dawson to Virginia. Coach Dawson's wife knew Coach Dawson was not on the plane; her emotional scene in the movie was fiction.

Coach Jackson and Assistant Coach Carl Kokor were not on the plane; they were at Penn State on a recruiting assignment.

Scene that was Hollywood scripted: The movie showed the players joking and laughing after a hard-fought 17—14 loss, but they would not have acted that way after such a loss; Coach Tolley was a very strict coach.

Scene that was Hollywood scripted: A rescue worker did not find a charred Marshall playbook at the crash scene that established the Marshall Football team as the victims. A Huntington Herald-Dispatch reporter, Jack Hardin, found a wallet belonging to John Young, a name that rang a bell with him. He called Ernie Salvatore at the paper, and Ernie confirmed that Young was on the team.

Scene that was Hollywood scripted: Reggie Oliver, the Marshall University quarterback, was shown paying his respects to three fallen teammates, his homeboys from Druid High School in a church in Tuscaloosa, Alabama. Actually, Oliver paid his respects to his four fallen teammates, Joe Hood, Bob Van Horn, Freddie Wilson, and Larry Sanders, in the Druid High School gym; the church would have been too small to accommodate all the mourners.

Scene that was Hollywood scripted: The scene in which Nate Ruffin walked into a board of governors meeting did not happen; Marshall didn't have such a board then. There were no "We Are Marshall" cheers that came from students outside the administration building, but Marshall later played up this theme.

Scene that was Hollywood scripted: Marshall University President Donald Dedmon referred most football-related tasks to the recently hired athletic director, the late Joe McMullen, who served at Penn State under Joe Paterno. McMullen, however, was not mentioned in the movie. The scriptwriters also failed to mention the late Ed Starling, the interim athletic director who led the program through difficult times after the crash. Starling made numerous contributions that were not recognized in the movie.

Scene that was Hollywood scripted: Reggie Oliver was playing wide receiver instead of quarterback because he was hampered by an elbow injury. Reggie was a drop—back quarterback who adjusted to Coach Lengyel's new offensive system, the option offense. Oliver made the adjustment very well and was selected for honorable mention on the All-America Team in 1973 at the quarterback position.

Scene that was Hollywood scripted: Coach Lengyel was not a clueless, scatterbrained coach. On the contrary, he was a smooth talker, very cerebral, and a natty dresser. He had excellent managing skills. He let the other coaches execute their plans and then would tweak everything to his liking.

Scene that was Hollywood scripted: Bill James, a former Marshall University basketball player who turned football player, was my teammate in 1972. He played until his eligibility was up and attempted to get a shot as an NFL wide receiver. The late Dave Smith was the basketball player who played on the Young Thundering Herd football team. "Big Dave" wasn't mentioned in the movie. Dave Smith should have been identified in the movie instead of Bill James.

Scene that was Hollywood scripted: The movie showed the late Terry Gardner catching a pass in the end zone. However, Terry actually scored the game-winning touchdown while running a screen pass in from the left side of the field. The real version was more dramatic than the Hollywood version.

Scene that was Hollywood scripted: Mr. Dedmon, who served as the interim Marshall University president, was not fired. He accepted a similar position at Radford after Marshall hired a permanent president.

At the end of the day, there were some hurt feelings among some of the people associated with the program.

WE ARE...

MARSHALL™

PREMIERE DINNER

HONORING THE 1971
YOUNG THUNDERING HERD
AND COACH JACK LENGYEL

MONDAY. DEC. 11.2006
7:00 PM
BIG GREEN ROOM.
JOAN C. EDWARDS STADIUM

CHAPTER TWENTY-TWO

HOW THE MARSHALL FOOTBALL PROGRAM ROSE FROM ASHES TO GLORY

When I arrived at Marshall as a member of the Young Thundering Herd in 1972, the ashes of the plane crash were still smoldering. I could not have imagined in my most optimistic dreams that its football program would enjoy history-making events recorded in the Huntington Herald-Dispatch.

1971: Young Thundering Herd Beats Xavier
Marshall rose up on September 25, 1971, to defeat
Xavier in its first home game following the plane crash.
Reggie Oliver passed to Terry Gardner for a touchdown
on the final play of the game in the 15—13 win.
Terry Gardner's scoring the winning touchdown against
Cincinnati Xavier

1984: Long String of Losing Ends
Marshall completed the 1984 season with consecutive
road wins at Illinois State and East Tennessee State
to finish with a 6—5 record. This was Marshall's first
winning season in 20 years.

1987: First Trip to the Playoffs
Marshall made its first NCAA Division I-AA playoff
appearance in 1987 and finished as the runner-up.
Northeast Louisiana defeated Marshall in the
championship game, 43—42, in Pocatello, Idaho.

1988: First SC Football Championship
NCAA Division I-AA player of the year Mike Barber
of Winfield, W.Va., led Marshall to its first Southern
Conference football championship. With an eight-game
win streak to begin the season, Marshall also climbed to
No. 1 in the nation for the first time.

1991: Marshall University Stadium Opens
Marshall had a banner year in 1991. Coach Jim
Donnan's team posted an 11−4 record and lost to
Youngstown State in the NCAA Division I-AA
playoff finals. The Thundering Herd opened Marshall
University Stadium with a 24−23 victory over New
Hampshire in front of a crowd of 33,116.

1992: NCAA Division I-AA Champions
Willy Merrick kicked the only field goal of his career
to beat Youngtown State, 31—28, and give Marshall
its first NCAA Division I-AA championship. Merrick
connected from 22 yards with 10 seconds left in the
game at Marshall University Stadium.

1996: Undefeated NCAA Division I-AA Champions
Head coach Bobby Pruett returned to his alma mater
with a bang, guiding Marshall to a 15−0 record and its
second NCAA Division I-AA championship. None
of the games was closer than two touchdowns. Pruett
received national coach of the year recognition.

1997: Moving into the Big Time
Randy Moss was a Heisman Trophy finalist in 1997
when Marshall made its NCAA Division I-A and Mid-
American Conference debut with 10 wins and a league
championship. Marshall opened the season with a loss at
West Virginia, 42-31.

1998: First Bowl Game Victory
Marshall knocked off South Carolina—its first win
against a Southeastern Conference opponent—on

the way to capturing the Mid-American Conference championship and earning a Motor City Bowl bid. Marshall then beat Louisville for its first bowl triumph.

1999: Winningest Team of the Decade
Marshall completed the decade of the 1990s with 114 victories, more than any other team in NCAA Division I-A or I-AA ever. Quarterback Chad Pennington was a Heisman Trophy finalist. Marshall defeated Western Michigan for the Mid-American Conference championship on a late Pennington pass to Eric Pinkerton.

2001: What a Game It Was
Quarterback Byron Leftwich led the Thundering Herd all the way back from a 30-point halftime deficit to beat East Carolina in the GMAC Bowl, 64 — 61, in double overtime. It was the highest-scoring bowl game in history. The teams combined for 1,141 total yards.

2002: MAC Champions, Won Bowl
Marshall capped another Mid-American Conference championship with a GMAC Bowl victory, but the season will be best remembered for offensive linemen carrying injured quarterback Byron Leftwich downfield between plays in the Akron game. Also, a Miami (Ohio) assistant coach was hauled away from Marshall Stadium by police after allegedly shoving a fan after a Thundering Herd victory.

2003: Full Steam into C-USA
Marshall announced it was leaving the Mid-American Conference to join Conference USA, but not without making headlines first. The Thundering Herd opened the season with an upset at No. 6 Kansas State. Marshall University Stadium was renamed in honor of school philanthropist Joan C. Edwards.

2004: End of an Era
Bobby Pruett retired as head coach at his alma mater
with a 94—23 record and an .803 winning percentage
for nine seasons. Pruett won more games than any
football coach in school history. His teams won five
Mid-American Conference championships, won the
NCAA Division I-AA championship in 1996 and went
to seven bowl games.

2005: Big Home Crowd Marks Season
A Joan C. Edwards Stadium record crowd of 36,914
turned out for the Kansas State game on Sept. 10, 2005.
K-State won, 21 — 19. Marshall compiled a 4—7 record
and was 3—5 as a first year member of Conference USA.

2006: We Are Marshall Movie Premiere
Warner Bros. Pictures film tells the story of the Marshall
University football team after a 1970 plane crashed
killed all 75 people aboard, including most of the team
members, coaching staff and many fans.

How MY LIFE WENT FROM ASHES TO GLORY

Herald-Dispatch
Sunday, April 17, 2005
Marshall honors notable alumni
Some honorees impressed with school's growth
by Curtis Johnson

HUNTINGTON—Marshall alumni young and old
turned out Saturday evening to eat, get reacquainted
with each other and recognize their peers for excellence.

The university's 68th Alumni Awards Banquet
culminated a weekend of alumni activities aimed at
show casing the university in the springtime, just weeks
away from graduation.

"We're really trying to showcase excellence in a number of different areas," said Lance West, vice president for alumni development for Marshall University. "Our ability to get the alumni association as visible as possible and get as many alumni and friends connected with the university is such a critical tool, especially when you're always in a period of trying to grow and get better."

Thirteen individuals and groups, including 106-year-old alumnus Emma Lene Harshbarger, were honored at the dinner held inside the student center's Don Morris Room.

Carolyne Brown, a 1969 Marshall graduate, said Saturday's dinner was the first she has attended in several years. It gave her a chance to support Marshall and the National Association for the Advancement of Colored People while seeing some old friends.

"I wanted to visit with people I haven't seen in a long, long time," she said. "It's great. We've just lost touch. You know how that goes. You know people lose touch over the years because they get so busy with their lives."

Harshbarger, of Milton, was the night's first honoree when the university recognized her as a "Daughter of Marshall." She's believed to be the school's oldest-living graduate.

Other winners were: Bob Cosmai, class of 1971, Distinguished Alumni award winner; Robert Shell, class of 1967, Distinguished Alumnus in Manufacturing; Sen. Bob Plymale, class of 1978, Distinguished Service Award; Bob Brammer, class of 1965, Distinguished Service Award ; Sylvia Ridgeway, class of 1976, Community Service Award; Sally Love, Community Service Award; Dr. Rudy Pauley, Dr. Carolyn Hunter Distinguished Faculty Service Award; Nicholas Slate, student, Herd Village Scholarship Award; Brittney Hughart, student, Herd Village Scholarship Award and the Boone County Friends of Marshall Club, club of the year.

Officials at the dinner said Gov. Joe Manchin was unable to attend due to a change in his schedule. He had originally scheduled to attend.

Earlier Saturday, black athlete alumni group Black Legends and other groups honored alumni during the Alumni Weekend Hall of Fame Award Extravaganza.

Dr. Phil Carter said the honorees were people who have been nurtured in Huntington and at Marshall University and have gone on to achieve national prominence. The group also recognized some local middle school students who are straight-A or honor roll students and are good at athletics, too, Carter said.

One of the alumni honorees, Les Hicks, one of 125 Black Legends, is a 1975 Marshall University graduate. Hicks was a linebacker and defensive end for the Herd team that went 2 — 9 and 4 — 7 in his two years at Marshall. He also received a graduate degree from MU in 1976.

"I'm very proud to be recognized," said Hicks, coordinator of pollution prevention and environmental resources at Lockheed Martin Aeronautics in Marietta, Ga. "I came (to MU) two years after the crash. I take great pride in building the foundation for what the program has become.

"I never envisioned the success Marshall would have," he said. "I never predicted all the buildings they have how."

Reprinted with permission of the Huntington Herald-Dispatch.

SPIRITUAL CONNECTION WITH SCOTTIE REESE

When I committed to Marshall University's Young Thundering Herd ll, I wasn't thinking about wins and losses. I was determined

246

to help Marshall revive its football program from ashes to glory regardless of the poll projections. Polls couldn't measure what's inside a man's heart. I was enamored with the thought of living my life vicariously for Scottie Reese.

Reese, a 5'-11", 185 pound linebacker and defensive end was undersized. However, he offset his physical deficiencies by using his quickness and intelligence effectively. I was inspired by his tragic loss while looking at a team picture outside the coaches' offices. In retrospect, my mind took me back to one of the country's most tragic plane crashes in American sports history. While I was coming to grips with the plan crash, I was saddened because Reese and others had been robbed of a full life. That's why I wanted to pick up where his life came to an abrupt end. It's hard to imagine how his parents coped with the loss of their son whom they described as lovable, intelligent, and friendly. They said that he never met a stranger. Reese, was one of six children born of Chester Sr. and Jimi in Waco, Texas. Every time I'd put my uniform on, I'd represent Scottie on and off the field in every conceivable aspect of my life. In return, I have received and enjoyed an infinite amount of glory on his behalf.

I thank Scottie for empowering me to make our journey from ashes to glory in one spirit. I gave the game of football everything that was inside of me.

I WAS FEATURED IN THE HUNTINGTON
HERALD-DISPATCH

Facts about my life and the book I wrote were featured article in the Herald-Dispatch as the November 14, 1970 crash victims were commemorated. My book, Against All Odds—4th Down and Forever, was introduced to the Herd nation by sports editor and former teammate Dave Walsh.

Although my parents could not read a book, their personal sacrifices enabled me to write one. Through hard work and sacrifice, I willed myself to learn in a household in which getting an education was not a focal point. My parents were not aware of the value of an education; hard work was the only thing they knew.

Hicks has heavy heart in remembering crash
by David Walsh
The Herald-Dispatch

Huntington—Lester Hicks heads to work. Wednesday at Lockheed Martin Aeronautics in Marietta, Ga., with a heavy heart.

Hicks will be thinking about Marshall University where his alma mater holds the annual plane crash memorial service at noon at Memorial Student Center. The ceremony honors the Thundering Herd players, coaches, staff, fans and flight crew—75 in all—who lost their lives on Nov. 14, 1970, when the chartered jet bringing the them back from a 17—14 loss at East Carolina earlier in the day crashed short of the runaway at Tri-State Airport in Kenova.

Hicks played for Coach Jack Lengyel and the Young Thundering Herd in 1972— 73. The 6-foot-5 defensive end came to Marshall after two years at Ellsworth Community College in Iowa Falls, Iowa.Hicks and his fellow teammates— surviving freshmen from the 1970 class who didn't make the fateful trip, walk-ons, athletes recruited from other sports and the first post-crash recruiting class—became one with the mission to revive a football program that had been all but wiped out by the greatest air disaster in sports history.

"That day will always be etched in my heart," Hicks said in a telephone interview from his home in Powder Springs, Ga. "I treat it like the loss of a family member.

Every time someone talks about it, my heart breaks. The guys who went before me made the ultimate sacrifice."

To some people, the Marshall Plane crash is a tragic footnote in sports history. To Hicks, it served as an inspiration to write a book about the event and how it inspired him to embrace a life of service. The title is, Against All Odds—4th Down and Forever: How the 1970 Marshall University Football Team Plane Crash Inspired Me. Hicks hoped to have the books out in time for the crash anniversary, but said they should be available in early December. He is planning to do a Huntington book signing.

"Insite," a corporate publication of Lockheed Martin Aeronautics, did an article on Hicks, an environmental safety engineer with Environmental, Safety and Health. Fellow employees and others — thanks to all the social media—either read or heard about that story and wanted to know more about Hicks and Marshall's rise from the ashes. Hicks later had a conversation with Dr. Marvin Mills, former safety department director at Marshall who is 91 and living in Lexington, Ky.

"Dr. Mills told me that he wanted me to write this book." Hicks said. "He said start writing it today." Hicks received a big assist from Craig T Greenlee, a Marshall graduate and former football player whose book about the Marshall plane crash—November Ever After—came out last year.

Hicks, 61, talks about experiences ranging from age 4 when he lived in Reynolds, Ga., and his father George worked as a sharecropper all the way to earning college degrees, raising a family, climbing the ladder in business and blossoming into a community leader.

He was a standout defensive end for Steubenville High School in 1969. Notre Dame, Ohio State, Nebraska, Pitt and other big-time schools made recruiting visits to the Ohio State steel town. So did Marshall, but he didn't measure up when it came to grades, so it was off to community college.

"I goofed off and it cost me," Hicks said.

As the first season at Ellsworth concluded, Hicks was in his room on that cold November night eating pizza and watching a football game when news about the Marshall Plane crash came across the screen.

"I was in shock," he sid. "It was gut-wrenching. Eighteen to 21-year-olds flying off to play a football game, their girl friends and family waiting for them. In minutes, life was gone. There was a lot of heartbreak everywhere."

Two quality seasons at Ellsworth meant Hicks had the big-time schools wanting him again. This time, Lengyel and the Young Thundering Herd won out over Notre Dame, Ohio State, Nebraska, Iowa State, Syracuse, and Dayton to name a few.

"Coach Lengyel was persistent," Hicks said. "He said. "I want you to be part of something. A lot of people want you, we need you. Step in and make a difference. I thought about what if I'd gone there (1970). I could have been on that team. To lose them then would have been very difficult."

During his recruiting visit to Marshall in 1972, Hicks said he was walking in Gullickson Hall and saw a picture of the crash victims. One player, defensive end Scottie Reese, got his attention. "I looked at the photo, saw Scottie Reese and said I want to play for him." Hicks said. "He's a lot like me. I could play for this guy."

While at Ellsworth, Hicks battled injuries. At Marshall, the injury bug struck again. A partially torn deltoid muscle forced Hicks to wear a shoulder harness for two seasons. He passed out during a weight lifting session his first season and later nearly died before he learned he had viral hepatitus. He said he considered suicide in 1972.

"My shoulder was constantly hurting and I was suffering with hepatitus. I felt like I let myself and my teammates down." Hicks said. "I was always tired and weary. I thought where is my life going? Nowhere."

Thank goodness for the talk Hicks had with Marshall Supporter Nick Diniaco. "He talked me out of it. I made the decision I wanted to live. I became the citizen that Diniaco encouraged me to be."

Hicks wore No. 80 and was known as the "Praying Mantis." He made yards tough to come by for opponents despite being undersized (212 pounds). Needless to say, Senior Day in 1973 was tough for Hicks. A 6—16 record for two years isn't what Hicks was used to.

"I let Scottie down," Hicks said. "I was never healthy. I didn't have my shoulder surgically repaired. That was not smart. However, I had a high threshold for pain. The competition kept getting better. You had to bring it or sit."

Marshall's down time in football continued until 1984 when the Thundering Herd won the final game that season at East Tennessee State to finish 6 — 5, its first winning record since 1964.

Championships in the Southern Conference and Mid-American Conference followed. Marshall won two NCAA Division I-AA national titles and was runner-up four times. The Herd went on to become the nation's winningest Division I program in the 1990s (114—25).

Victories in six of eight bowl games, a No. 10 national ranking in 1999 after going undefeated, three Heisman Trophy candidates in wide-out Randy Moss and quarterbacks Chad Pennington and Byron Leftwich, and former Herd players suiting up for Super Bowl champions led by Troy Brown with three rings while with the New England Patriots.

Hicks said having a part in helping the dreams become reality makes those days of playing in pain and making sacrifices worth it.

"Johnathan Goddard (former Herd linebacker who died in 2008 from injuries suffered in a motocycle accident) was my favorite player. I loved his motor. I loved his heart."

Hicks said he got inspiration early in life from his mother Clifford Simmons Hicks, who died on Mother's Day in 1966. She was 51. He was one of 14 children and the first to go to college.

"Her passion fueled my fire," he said. "She literally worked herself to death. Football was my ticket out."

Adversity followed Hicks after he left Marshall. He had a near-fatal blood clot after a knee scope in 1992. And he was almost killed in a car crash in 2005, and later that year, suffered a ruptured appendix.

Hicks returned to the campus in October 2011 for a reunion of teams from the early 1970's. Hicks and the Young Herd also got attention from the 2006 movie "We are Marshall" that made the world aware of one of the greatest comeback stories of all time.

In 2005, Marshall University's Black Legends named Hicks as one of its 125 Most Impactful Black Athletes of the 20th Century.

On Feb.23, 2012, the Marietta Diversity Council and the African American Leadership Forum (AALF) held the 2012 Black History Month Celebration with a special employee recognition Lockheed Martin employees honored. He was recognized for achievement in Sports/Community Service. He's been with the company 28 years.

Hicks met his wife, Della, who is from Charleston, while he was at Marshall. They have a son, Brian, and three daughters, LeShea, Tiffany, and Shante. Hicks is actively engaged in the community, pouring the benefit of his experiences into others' lives on multiple fronts.

He serves as a mentor to troubled youth, teaches Sunday school to 4-to-7-year-old children, serves on the Cobb County (Ga.) Literacy Council to decrease the dropout rate and to improve literacy in the county and contacts colleges for prospective student-athletes if they first make it in the classroom.

Yes, Hicks admits he will have mixed emotions Wednesday. Sorrow for the 75 individuals who had their lives cut way too short in his eyes. For the rise that university and that town has made from that dark day, the opportunity that university afforded a student-athlete and the tools it provided to help frame his character and prepare him to touch the lives of others through service and mentoring.

. . . grateful says it all.

Reprinted with permission of the Huntington Herald-Dispatch.

CHAPTER TWENTY-THREE

MY LIFE TODAY

I have had an incredible life. Like the little girl with the curl—when life was good, it was very good. On the other hand, when it was bad, it was very bad. However, surviving is in my DNA; it's what I saw my parents do throughout their lives of lack and struggle. By watching them and others, I learned how to make things happen.

I was just blessed with a sense of progressive activism. Progressive activism demands that you never settle for what you have accomplished, so I never settled just for my last accomplishment—I always pushed myself to reach for more.

The poorest person in today's society is the one without a dream. My dream of playing football for the Steubenville Big Red became a reality that exceeded my wildest dreams. On September 28, 2012, my former high school made me honorary captain at a homecoming game versus Pittsburgh Westinghouse, and I did the coin toss to start it off. The public school superintendent, Mike McVey, Nate Freeman, a longtime friend and booster president, and the coaching staff treated my wife and me like royalty. An electronic billboard at the stadium read, "Welcome Les & Della Hicks, Class of '70 and #84." Athletic director Fred Heatherington gave us tickets to the game and reserved parking. Reno Saccoccia asked me to give a pre-game pep talk, and he and I led the team onto the field. The athletic department gave me access to the new press box dedicated to the memory

255

of my former coach, the late Abe Bryan. My former coaches
Mike Herrick and Tom Gardner and the coach's son, Tom Tom
congratulated me after the coin toss ceremony.

40 Years Later
Hicks recounts life as a "Young Thundering Herd"
September 1, 2012
by Ed Looman sports correspondent
The Herald Star

Steubenville—During his high school playing days,
Lester Hicks was known as a fierce defensive end. Soon,
he will be known for authoring the fourth book on the
tragic Marshall University plane crash.

Hicks, a 1970 Big Red graduate, was in town Friday
for alma mater's homecoming game with Pittsburgh
Westinghouse. He served as honorary captain. Hicks

played for Abe Bryan and was a member of the 1969 Steubenville team that went 7 — 2 — 1 and battled Massillon to a scoreless tie.

Following graduation, Hicks took his gridiron talents to Ellsworth College in Iowa. From there, he moved to Marshall.

Hicks, a member of the Marshall program in 1972 and 1973, teams that took on the staggering task of re-establishing football at the school. He was a 6 — 5 defensive end on what was the second edition of the "Young Thundering Herd."

"When Jack Lengyel, the Marshall Head coach, recruited me, he said, 'other schools may want you, but we need you.' It was then that I decided I needed to be at Marshall," Hicks noted.

He joined an eclectic group of athletes recruited from other sports, along with surviving freshmen players who didn't make the fateful trip, and a host of walk-ons. Their task wasn't so much to win championships, but to simply play competitively and position for future success.

Along the way, the program endured its lumps, recording consecutive 2 — 9 seasons in 1971 and 1972 before managing a slight improvement to 4 — 7 in 1973. In an effort to get the program off the ground, Hicks and his teammates made their fair share of sacrifices, gaining perspective along the way.

"I learned to sacrifice my talent for the betterment of the team by playing hurt and almost playing every position, including defensive tackle at 212 pounds, which probably cost me a potential career in the National Football League," he said. "On the football field, I worked as if I was to play for 100 years, and I prayed as if I was to die tomorrow."

On November 14, 1970, the lives of 75 people were lost in the worst single air tragedy in NCAA sports history. Among the losses were nearly the entire Marshall Football team, coaches, flight crew, numerous fans and supporters.

Lengyel was hired following the crash and the initial "Young Thundering Herd" took the field in 1971.

For most people, the crash is simply a tragic footnote in sports history, as well as the subject of the 2006 movie, "We Are Marshall." For Hicks, who resides in Powder Springs, Ga., with his wife Della, it is part of his life story. He returned to the Huntington campus last October when the school held a 40th anniversary reunion honoring Hicks and his teammates.

This event allowed him to renew the bond that he shares with his former teammates and prompted him to write the book. He began his work in February and hopes to have the book released on November 14. His work will be entitled Against All Odds—4th Down and Forever.

During his time at Marshall and in the years to follow, Hicks, who returned to Harding Stadium for only the second time in 42 years, faced his share of adversity. He nearly died after passing out during a weight training session in college due to undetected viral hepatitis. He had a near-fatal blood clot after a knee scope in 1992. And he was almost killed in a car crash in 2005, and later that year, suffered a ruptured appendix.

Those travails, as well as the memory of those who perished in the aircraft accident in 1970, taught him to treasure each moment and each breath.

"I personally have learned that life is fragile," he said "The loss of the players' lives taught me to never take life for granted, regardless of my age. I felt privileged to be a Marshall University football player, and I felt an obligation to play through frustration, fatigue and a partially torn deltoid.

"I learned not to complain about anything because millions would love to have the good and the bad of my life. I treat each day as if it is my last day of living. As a result, I accomplish what I can by not leaving anything for tomorrow."

In a summary about the book, Tiffany Hicks writes that her father's journey echoes the universal sentiment that you can beat the odds as long as you have faith, determination, discipline and a tireless pursuit of happiness.

"This book takes the reader on an insightful ride of heartbreak, triumph and perseverance," she notes. "In a time of despair, division and recession, a book like this is just what the doctor ordered because it's relatable and its message of hope and generosity transcends race, gender and/or age."

Reprinted with permission of the Steubenville Herald Star.

The day my family and I arrived in Steubenville, neighbors jeered us because we were poor people from Reynolds, Georgia. Forty-two years later, the town welcomed me, a resident of Powder Springs, Georgia with open arms. Back then, I didn't have any clothes. In 1955, I discovered that no matter what you do, some people are not going to accept you. I learned that a lot of heartache and pain could be minimized by ignoring what others said about me. The more I was ridiculed, the more blessings I received. Today, through hard work and perseverance, my wife and I have acquired many of life's finer things.

MY HEALTH

I remember when my parents could not afford to take us to see a doctor. Today, I am blessed to have specialists treating me from head to toe and keeping illness away by the power of God. I thank God for blessing me with my doctors, who have become an integral part of my life. I know that God is working through the minds and hands of the following accomplished specialists:

Dr. Stephan Palte, Internal Medicine
The late Dr. Kapsch, Vascular Surgeon
Dr. Tantaran, Internal Medicine
Dr. Seth Rosen, Colorectal Surgeon
Dr. Thomas Emersom, Urologist
Dr. Aris Iatridis, Breathing and Sleep Disorder
Dr. David Gower, Neurologist
Dr. Raul Oyola, Oncologist
Dr. Aasim Shiekh, Gastrointestinal Medicine
Dr. Mini Gupta, Nephrologist and Hypertension
Dr. Michael Christa, Primary Care Physician
Dr. Kirk Howling, Primary Care Physician
Martricia Turner, Nurse Practitioner
Della Lertpenmaeta, Nurse Practitioner
Toni Clarke, Referral Specialist

Della and I are like old Timex watches—we take a licking but keep on ticking. There are mornings when I have struggled to get out of bed because I'm hurting so badly. What's more, there are days when I don't want to talk because my decrepit jaws are so tight. However, after I make it to the shower, I put all my aches and pains behind me. I walk three to five hours every day at work and jog three miles every other day; I was raised to be tough and resilient.

I speak God's blessings upon us. My wife and I look like the picture of health. I have learned to shake my illnesses off by keep moving. I always believed that if I stopped, I might not be able to get my body started again, but whenever I start moving,

I don't stop until bedtime. Although my wife is awaiting knee replacement surgery in the near future, she is healed of the Lord.

I'm a positive thinker. What we believe affects the outcome. I have internalized the belief that the power of life and death is on our tongue. Regardless of the circumstances, I know that with God's favor, I will prevail.

DELLA

Delia and I will always be complete opposites. However, there's a three-fold cord binding us together, so we were able to live fruitful and productive lives together through compromise. She is the most laid-back and caring woman I've ever met, and she's always had my best interests at heart. When I wasn't able to help myself, she bathed me, dressed me, and carried me until I was able to take care of myself again. As fate would have it, I did the same for her when she was bedridden. She has been an excellent role model for our daughters.

My Family

Les and Della displaying Marshall University Black Alumni Legend's 1 of 125 Most Impactful Athlete Award in 2005

Tiffany and LeShea

LeShea Dionne

LeShea is a fun-loving extrovert who puts the needs of others above her own. She served in the U.S. Navy until she received an honorable medical discharge. LeShea holds three degrees and is currently working on a master degree. Her goal is to be a coroner. She has three sons, Deion, Donaveen, and Camden.

Brian Les

Brian is a quick-thinking intellectual who had one of the highest IQ test scores among his age group. His athletic ability could have exceeded my talent. I regret that I got some bad advice regarding restricting him from participation in athletics while attending high school. It was a decision we deeply regret. He is an outstanding poet. Brian is a very loyal friend. He is a highly sought-after DJ throughout the Atlanta metropolitan area.

Christian Tiffany

Tiffany is a young lady mature beyond her years. She is a multitalented professional waiting for her career to explode in telecommunications with an emphasis on journalism. She was lauded as one of the best writers by one of her Georgia State professors in Atlanta and has almost earned a second degree from the Art Institute of Pittsburgh in Web design. She graduated in the top third of her high school and college classes.

Shanté Nicole

Shanté was recently married to Robert Polite, who has earned multiple firefighter awards for bravery on the job. Shanté is a very intelligent, deep thinker working toward a nursing degree, and she and Robert are first time parents of Lexie Brianna, born December 19, 2012.

GRANDCHILDREN

Deion Shaunkese

Deion has a positive outlook on life. He possesses a great deal of untapped potential, and he's someone who throws caution to the wind. He has the heart of a lion and a passion for sports. When he discovers that life is all about making compromises, he'll be very successful in sports, but most important in life.

Donaveen Jai Ruff

Donaveen is a quiet young man who is always respectful of his elders. His demeanor remains calm regardless of the circumstances. Donaveen is loner who likes to watch wrestling and prepare meals for his grandfather, Steve. He adapts to change very well.

Camden Darell Henderson and Mother LeShea

Camden is a one-year-old who skipped the infant stage of his life and fast-forwarded himself to the toddler stages. He is truly a happy baby who learns very quickly. We are amazed how well he grasps things. Like most babies, Camden brightens our days.

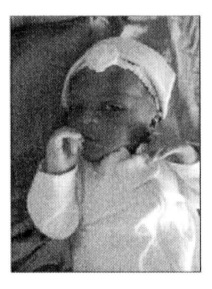

Lexie Briana, the first daughter of Robert and Shante' Polite

MY FAITH

When I was four, I could not have imagined how blessed I would be at sixty-one. Faith is the substance of things hoped for and the evidence of things not seen. Without faith, I couldn't have accomplished the things that will define my legacy. My faith has given me hope for the future. In the absence of hope, I could have committed suicide on two occasions; however, even in the midst of my despair, I know it was God telling me to choose life.

MY PASTOR

My wife and I have matured in our faith over time. Whenever we recognized that a church we were attending didn't coincide with the Word of God, we were out of there. When Della and I were once looking for a church home, Tammie Ellis, a parent of one of her students invited us to her church, Covenant Christian Ministries, where the presiding pastor was Frederick T Anderson. We liked Pastor Anderson's mission for the ministry, to perfect the saints by walking in a covenant relationship with God while being a light to others (exemplifying godly character), opening blind eyes (enabling them to see the things freely promised to them by the Word of God), and freeing people from the bonds of sin, tradition, and lifestyle through practical application of the taught Word. We joined this church, sensing that his mission was to win souls to Christ in lieu of fame and fortune. Our spirituality has grown exponentially under Pastor and Mrs. Anderson's leadership.

Pastor Anderson has taught the Word with boldness, clarity and accuracy, and he lives what he preaches. Covenant Christian Ministries was voted the number one faith-based church with 500 members or less in the Atlanta metro area in 2005. Pastor Anderson has a passion for the ministry and people; next to his family, they are his life.

Pastor Anderson and I are kindred spirits.
* We both moved to Georgia in July 1984.
* Our wives are speech pathologists.
* Both of our parents had fourteen children
* Our parents are from the South.
* He attended Syracuse University, where I could have gone on a football scholarship.
* We always present ourselves in a professional manner
* We like the same food.
* We married our wives the same month.
* We give more than we receive.
* We believe in excellence.

CHAPTER TWENTY-FOUR

LIFE IS TOO LEGIT TO QUIT

My life epitomizes Murphy's Law; everything that could go wrong, it did go wrong. Sometimes, I felt as if Job and I were brothers. Like Job, I have walked through the fire, but survived every time. At times, when the weight of my problems was too much for my shoulders, God miraculously parted the proverbial Red Sea for me.

My hope has usually been internal. When it was external, I thought suicide was the answer. Therefore, here's my advice: Refrain from negative thinking and stay active — an idle mind is the devil's workshop. Don't be upset about circumstances. Be determined to walk through the difficult times to victory. Believe that God has a bright future for you. It doesn't matter if you don't have as much education as someone else. It doesn't matter how influential your family was or is. It doesn't matter what your background was — just don't ever give up, because quitters never win. When you quit for the first time, it's much easier to quit the next time, and then it becomes a habit. I always refused to quit. Every great accomplishment starts with that internal decision from within: I will try.

This poem, which I first came across at Marshall, defines my life.

INVICTUS

Out of the night that covers me
Black as the pit from pole to pole.
I thank whatever gods (The Father, The Son,
and The Holy Ghost) may be
For my unconquerable soul.

In the fell clutch of circumstance
I have not winched nor cried aloud.
Under the bludgeoning of chance
My head is bloody, but unbowed.

Beyond this place of wrath and tears
Looms but the Horror of the shade.
And yet the menace of the years
Finds and shall find me unafraid.

It matters not how strait the gate,
How charged with punishments the scroll.
I am the master of my fate:
I am the captain of my soul.

— Anonymous

SPECIAL THANKS

I give special thanks to Craig T Greenlee, the only living link with a connection to the Herd's undefeated freshman team of '68. He played on the Marshall Football team in '69. If you want to know the true story about the football team's fate, read his November Ever After, which has received outstanding reviews and can be purchased online at Amazon.com or at bookstores. It's a must-read for sports fans and those who root for the underdog.

Craig afforded me many hours of his invaluable time giving me guidance about authoring this book. He and I attended Marshall University concurrently for two years. Although we traveled in different circles and were members of different fraternities, he has been a true friend and a brother. Moreover, he also tried to help one of my daughters, Tiffany, a journalist and a social media professional, find employment. Tiffany, a highly skilled professional, is waiting for her big break. She will bless the employer who takes a chance on her.

The late Mrs. Orlea Howard, like my mother gave me love and protection. She treated me like one of her sons. I think about her often.

In actuality, my wife, Della is the co-author of this project. She spent as many hours as I researching, typing, scanning and proofreading the manuscript for nine consecutive months that it took to complete "Against All Odds—4th Down and Forever". In regards to motivation, she kept me focused and enthused. Della is my best friend, my hero, and my one true love. As I was immersed in this project, she challenged me while making me laugh like no one else. She is my kiss of Heaven who continuously blesses our family. I sincerely thank my wife for the time, energy and the love that was demonstrated throughout this rewarding process.

Likewise, our daughter, Tiffany played an integral role in the production of this project as well. She also spent countless hours ensuring that the book met literary expectations. She also serves as my publicist. Tiffany introduced us to Facebook, Twitter, Pinterest, and other social media outlets. She keeps us abreast of the "now Generation". Her love and devotion assisting us with the writing of this project will always be remembered.

The plane crash that killed seventy-five players, coaches, flight crew, and Marshall fans on November 14, 1970, is a tragic footnote in sports history and the subject of the 2006 movie We Are Marshall.

Hicks, a former player, tells how he handled the pressure of being recruited by suitors representing numerous storied college football programs nationwide.

Surprisingly, he chose Marshall over the country's elite football programs to be part of the post-crash recruiting class, the Young Thundering Herd II.

He recalls the emotional strain and commitment necessary to help revive Marshall's football program. What's more, he introduces his phenomenal parents, George and Clifford Hicks, to the world. His parents and the crash victims gave him inspiration to embrace a life of service.

A countless number of co-workers who either read or heard about his connection with the tragic event urged him to write more about his and Marshall's rise from ashes to glory.

Against All Odds provides the reader with a compelling account regarding the events leading up to his suicidal thoughts. His friend unknowingly convinced Hicks that he had many reasons to live. After getting a second chance at life, he responded by dedicating the rest of his life playing in the honor of one of the crash victims, Scottie Reese who played his position.

Hicks proclaims that he works and plays as if he were going to live for a hundred years and prays as if he were going to die the next day. As result, he played with a partially torn deltoid for two years and unknowingly with hepatitis.

In spite of insurmountable odds, he earned three college degrees with honors, raised four children and climbed the ladder in business and blossomed into a community leader. His journey echoes the universal sentiment that you can beat the odds if you have faith, determination, discipline, and a tireless desire to pursue happiness.

The book takes the reader in an insightful ride of heartbreak, triumph, and perseverance in times of despair, division, and poverty.

Les Hicks cashed in on his football talent by attracting prominent suitors from the Big Ten, Big Eight, Pac Ten, Notre Dame, Maryland, Syracuse and others.

He earned an associate of arts degree from Ellsworth Community College and a bachelor of arts and a Master of Science degree from Marshall University. He made the dean's list several times and was listed in Who's Who among Students in American Junior Colleges.

Hicks, a senior environmental safety engineer, has been with Lockheed Martin Aeronautics Company for twenty-eight years. His experience at Marshall cultivated life lessons that he brings to work each day, and in fact drove him to his career choice. He chose the safety profession because he said that there were no trade secrets in the profession. Hicks believes that the safety profession is a humanistic way of extending godly love to the workforce by helping them return home the same way they came to work. He is very passionate about strictly enforcing safety rules because his father lost an eye while working on a job, and he had a childhood friend killed in the workplace.

He earned twenty-one awards from the State of Georgia, including a first-place award for his anti-litter campaign and a third-place award for his pollution prevention efforts during an eight-year period. He has been on the front page of the Atlanta

Business Chronicle and has been featured in national news and advertising publications. He has made presentations on safety, recycling, and energy conservation to audiences from all over the United States and abroad.

Hicks is active in the community, pouring the benefit of his experiences into other lives on multiple fronts. He serves as a mentor to troubled youth, teaches Sunday school, serves on the Cobb County Literacy Council to decrease the dropout rate and improve literacy in his county.

In his wallet, Hicks keeps a lifetime pass to all Marshall University athletic events, a reward he and his teammates received for their crucial role in reestablishing the football program. It's a fitting visual reminder for Hicks, who maintains an emotional tie to Coach Lengyel, the program, and the university that did so much for his character and prepared him to touch the lives of others through service and mentoring.

Hicks and his wife, Della, are the proud parents of four who have also earned multiple college degrees with honors.